BIG QUESTIONS IN CREATIVITY 2018

BIG QUESTIONS IN CREATIVITY 2018

Edited by
Kristin Fields
Cynthia Burnett
& Marie Mance

A Collection of First Works, Volume 6

ICSC Press
International Center for Studies in Creativity
Buffalo State, The State University of New York
Buffalo, NY, U.S.A.

ICSC Press
**INTERNATIONAL CENTER *for*
STUDIES *in* CREATIVITY**

BUFFALO STATE • The State University of New York

ICSC Press
International Center for Studies in Creativity
Buffalo State, The State University of New York
1300 Elmwood Avenue
Buffalo, NY 14222, USA
icscpress.com

© 2018 by ICSC Press

ISBN: 978-0-9849795-9-2 (print edition)

Library of Congress Control Number: 2013907967

Simultaneously published in multiple formats, both print and electronic. For alternative versions and to discover other titles, visit icscpress.com.

Book Design and Graphics: Kevin D. Opp

All trademarks are the property of their respective owners.

While the authors and editors have made every effort to provide accurate Internet addresses at the time of publication, the publisher, editors, or authors do not assume responsibility for changes that occur after publication. Further, the publisher does not control and does not assume any responsibility for author or third-party websites or their content.

This book is dedicated to the memory of
Dr. Mary Murdock (1947-2010).

In her time at the ICSC, she instilled
bravery and curiosity to explore big questions,
and inspired so many to spread and
encourage the spirit of creativity.

Contents

Introduction   1

Organizational Creativity

How Can Creativity Enhance Self-Managed Organizations?
Ingrid De Clercq   7

Is Female Leadership the Key to Unlocking Organizational Creativity?
Pamela Z. H. Pauwels   23

Why Do Nonprofits Need Creativity and How Might Creativity Differ in Nonprofit Organizations?
Alice F. Jacobs   35

Creativity and Education

What is the Relationship Between Creativity and Learning?
Sara Smith   49

Is Self-Directed Education the Answer to the Creativity Crisis?
Nicole Colter   63

Creative Process

How Might Emergent Thinking Bridge the Gap Between Divergent and Convergent Thinking Throughout the Creative Problem Solving Process?
Brian D. Kalina   81

What Does It Take to Tolerate Ambiguity? A Search Into Love, Happiness, and Balance
Anneke Veenendaal-de Kort   91

Creativity and Life Circumstance

What Impact Does Multiple Sclerosis Have on the Ability to Engage in Creativity?
Danielle Myers   107

Can Creativity Help Children in Foster Care Transition From Surviving to Thriving?
Emilie Kenneally   123

Are Individuals in Poverty More Creative?
Cher Ravenell   133

Acknowledgments   147

About the Editors   148

About the International Center for Studies in Creativity   150

About ICSC Press   151

Introduction

> "Do not follow where the path may lead.
> Go instead where there is no path and leave a trail."
>
> Ralph Waldo Emerson

The study and pursuit of creativity are grounded in the fluidity of the subject. Many have made their mark in the field through expressing their own personal "creativity and...", completing the statement with topics that ignite internal passion and curiosity.

The students who have walked through the doors of the International Center for Studies in Creativity (ICSC) over its 50-year history have entered with their own "creativity and...." They followed a newly discovered path and an academic journey that examined creativity in its purest and most honest forms. After that foundation was set, they were able to reintroduce their "and", and view it through a new lens.

Each year, the ICSC asks its students to identify a *big question* they would like to explore. This book is the resultant research of ten students whose passion and curiosity has led them to delve into new areas in the field of creativity. The path carved by the forefathers and foremothers of the study of creativity has taken these individuals as far as it can; they are now their own trailblazers, pulling from personal experience and in-depth research to continue to move the field forward.

In this, the 6th edition of the *Big Questions in Creativity* anthology, four themes emerged from the essays: organizational creativity, creativity and education, creative process, and creativity and life circumstance.

Organizational Creativity

The paradigm of the workplace, historically perceived as a commute to an office with set hours of operation, has recently seen significant disruption with the introduction and acceptance of such practices as flexible scheduling, unlimited vacation time and telecommuting. The authors in this section explore what role creativity holds within the modern workplace.

Ingrid De Clercq explores the self-managed organization, a hierarchy-free organizational model that is driven by matching project need and employee expertise, demonstrating how infusing creative leadership, practice and deliberate tools can further enhance team collaboration and overall organizational success. Pamela Pauwels explores the characteristics of leaders through the lens of gender, specifically examining the disparity of women who hold key leadership roles as well as the impact of gender diversity within the C-suite. Alice Jacobs takes a more specific examination of nonprofit organizations, highlighting how the differing business models of nonprofit and for-profit utilize creativity and innovation, and how the constructs and responsibilities of nonprofits require a creative skill and mindset.

Creativity and Education

Businesses are more often citing creativity and creative problem solving as highly valued skills of its workforce—so how might we best infuse this mindset within educational constructs to best prepare our youth for the future? Sara Smith explores the misconception of many educators that the classroom does not afford time for creativity. She posits the interwoven nature of creativity and learning, and offers recommendations to integrate creativity into the classroom experience. Nicole Colter addresses the creativity crisis in America, offering self-directed education as a viable solution.

Creative Process

The authors in this section take a deeper exploration of the components of the creative process. The formal Creative Problem Solving (CPS) process takes participants through the dichotomous thinking of divergence and convergence. Brian Kalina describes a new form of creative thinking that offers a scaffold for the exploration of ideas—he calls this *emergent thinking* and offers a fresh set of guidelines for facilitators to use. Anneke Veenendaal de Kort delves into a foundational skill for creative thinking—tolerance for ambiguity—and identifies what qualities are required to successfully express this skill.

Creativity and Life Circumstance

The mindset and skillset surrounding creativity are assets in navigating through circumstances thrust upon humanity. Danielle Myers shares her personal experiences in addition to an in-depth exploration of how those diagnosed with multiple sclerosis can find opportunities to engage with creativity. Emilie Kenneally examines creativity as an essential skill for survival and a way for a healthy transition into adulthood for children living in foster care. Cher Ravenell examines creativity through the lens of poverty, considering if individuals in dire economic circumstances exhibit greater creativity than that of their more monetarily comfortable counterparts.

Conclusion

The Big Questions in this collection represent the consideration of humanity combined with possibility. The authors have embraced curiosity as their guide, and have skillfully woven theory with practice. In reading each author's essay, you will be swept into their journey for answers, and hopefully left inspired to strike out on your own trail of discovery.

Kristin Fields
Cynthia Burnett
Marie Mance

Buffalo, N.Y.

ORGANIZATIONAL CREATIVITY

How Can Creativity Enhance Self-Managed Organizations?

Ingrid De Clercq

International Center for Studies in Creativity
SUNY Buffalo State

Abstract

Recently we have seen a rise in self-managed organizations. Frustrated by the inertia caused by hierarchy, or eager to deploy the full potential of their work force, enlightened leaders have transformed their companies' structures and practices. New organizational frameworks and methodologies have emerged: some still in the experimental phase, others already well established, all reducing hierarchical layers and promoting self-management. This paper attempts to unveil the role of creativity in this kind of organizational model. Using a layered approach to creativity, this paper will demonstrate in what ways creativity and creative leadership can be an answer, an added value, or even a necessity to the self-managed organizations' nature and needs.

How Can Creativity Enhance Self-Managed Organizations?

In spite of the unprecedented progress of the last two centuries, we notice a growing feeling of disengagement—mainly but not exclusively in larger corporations. Workers show up with their bodies but not with their hearts. There is a feeling of discontentment, powerlessness, and an inability to meet growing expectations as well as the pressure to perform. And this feeling runs through the entire organization.

In 2012, Towers Watson, an HR consulting company, measured employee engagement of 32,000 workers in the corporate sector in 29 countries. They found that only 35% of the workers were feeling engaged in their work, 22% were feeling unsupported and lacking energy, and a staggering 43% were feeling detached or actively disengaged (Towers Watson, 2012). Why might this be the case? There are several possible reasons, but one of them is hierarchy (Hamel, 2013). We live in a complex world, with an ever-increasing pace of change. High levels of complexity combined with a slow decision process leads to low involvement as workers wait for their higher-ups to make decisions, and are in the meantime steering blind (Laloux, 2014). Gary Hamel (2013) formulated this concept very well: "Traditional pyramidal structures demand too much of too few and not enough of everyone else" (para. 2).

One of the consequences of corporate hierarchies is an increasing number of employees on sick leave because of physical and mental collapse caused by overwork or stress, known as burnout. In Belgium alone, burnout has risen 60% between 2009 and 2014 (Stichting Innovatie & Arbeid, 2014). It seems that the command-and-control management model, a relic of the Industrial Revolution, no longer harmonizes well with a world where information moves at the speed of light. Former Chaparral Steel CEO Gordon Forward stated that many CEOs are managing for the 3%: they are creating rules to control the small number of nonconforming employees who might misuse their autonomy, while suppressing the innovation and creativity of the 97% who just want to do a good job (Carney & Getz, 2009). This way of managing organizations seems increasingly out of date.

Emergence of a New Way of Working

In the book *Reinventing Organizations*, Laloux (2014) described how humanity evolves in stages and how, at every stage, we make a leap in our abilities: cognitively, morally, and psychologically. We develop a new set of values, needs, motivations, morals, worldviews, and organizational models. The trigger for a leap comes from a major life challenge that cannot be solved using the current world view. Laloux's (2014) theory is that a new shift in consciousness is currently taking place, leading to the invention of new organizational models. Chris Rufer, the founder and president of self-managed company Morning Star, said the following about the structure of self-managing organizations:

> Clouds form and then go away because atmospheric conditions, temperatures, and humidity cause molecules of water to either condense or vaporize. Organizations should be the same; structures need to appear and disappear based on the forces that are acting in the organization. When people are free to act, they're able to sense those forces and act in ways that fit best with reality. (Hamel, 2011, para. 56)

Structures and Practices

Most self-managed organizations are structured in teams of up to 15 people, called "circles" at companies such as HolacracyOne (Robertson, 2016) and Semco (Semler, 1993), or squads, tribes, guilds, and chapters at Spotify (Kniberg & Ivarsson, 2012). The fundamentals of autonomous self-management are embedded into every process undertaken by self-managed organizations and teams. Below are some of the most important practices, presented to illustrate the impact of self-management on worker engagement (Bakke, 2005; Colman, de Caluwé, Dendooven, & van Landuyt, 2015; Kirkpatrick, 2014; Laloux, 2014; Robertson, 2016; Semler, 1993):

Self-chosen roles. Rather than having a boss telling you what to do, you decide for yourself what you want to work on and where you can make the greatest contribution. Once the commitment is made, you need to deliver. Valve Software's (2012) handbook stated, "You were not hired to fill a specific job description, but to constantly look around for the most valuable work you could be doing" (p. 9).

Autonomous decision making. There is no formal hierarchy, only a natural one. You are responsible for the domain of work that you've chosen, and within your zone of competence and responsibility you can make any decision, unless it impacts others. In that case you need to seek advice from everyone meaningfully affected, and/or people with expertise in the matter. No colleague, whatever their importance, can tell a decision-maker what to decide. Leaders form naturally once people start following them.

Internal and external hiring. Hiring is done by the team itself. Focus is on a potential hiree's fit with the organization and its purpose. New teams and new roles easily form when there is a need.

Compensation and promotion. Salaries are self-set with peer calibration. A fluid rearrangement of roles replaces traditional promotions and job titles.

Performance management. There is a strong focus on team performance, with peer-based processes for individual appraisals and team evaluation.

Conflict management. It is every employee's responsibility to speak up and deliver honest feedback. A multi-step conflict resolution process begins first within the team, then with a facilitator, and only at the latest instance with the CEO.

Purchasing. There is no central purchasing department. When you need something, you order it, or take it from the stock. If in doubt, you ask advice.

Some of these practices of self-managed companies may seem revolutionary, but there are groups already functioning like this that have been working effectively for quite some time. Consider the development of the Linux open source software: everyone can pitch in, everyone can kill a bad idea, anyone can lead, no one can dictate, one can easily build on top of what others have done, excellence usually wins (and mediocrity doesn't), and great contributions are recognized and celebrated (Hamel, 2012). Wikipedia uses similar practices.

Hopes and Fears

Unfortunately, something that sounds like a good idea can be challenging to implement. Jean-François Zobrist (2007), the charismatic leader of the French company Favi stated, "Bringing a company from traditional to self-managing, is creating a disruption, followed by many mini-disruptions, and needs to be done in total coherence, flanked with some simple values" (p. 134). Daniel Tenner (2017) of GrantTree confirmed that self-management does not emerge naturally from the removal of management—it takes discipline and great structures.

Teams at neighborhood nursing organization Wit-Gele Kruis sometimes struggle to set their own key performance indicators (KPIs): some are too ambitious, some are not ambitious enough (Colman et al., 2015). When the perfect balance was finally struck, one of the nurses stated:

> Honestly, in the beginning I thought: it was better before. But now I definitely don't want to go back to the old situation! Our team is much smaller, ensuring good collegiality. There's sometimes friction, but we learn to handle it. (Colman et al., 2015, p. 171)

My own experience in assisting the Belgian IT company Irisnet taught me that giving each other feedback is a major hurdle. Also, being responsible for a domain of work within a company is well appreciated, but can leave people at a loss for how to organize. Irisnet's Tempo Team, created to speed up the implementation, started to realize the importance of shared values and mindset once there were fewer rules.

Making decisions autonomously is not easy, but it can be necessary. For example, at GrantTree, workers sought too much advice before making a decision, which dragged out the entire decision-making process (Tenner, 2016).

What Can Creativity Mean for These Organizations?

Working to complete a master's degree in creativity while simultaneously introducing these new concepts at an IT company in Brussels made me realize that there is a huge potential that has not yet been explored well enough. There is plenty of scientific research on how self-leadership and self-managing teams enhance innovation and creativity, but hardly anything on how creativity can enhance self-management. This section aims to show that relationship by taking an empirical approach. Much like Dennis Bakke (2005), CEO of AES, said: "We try things out in practice and then see if it works in theory" (p. 158).

To show the relationship, I'd like to use a layered approach by identifying creativity as a *tool box,* a *skill set,* and a *mindset.* The tool box, with creative tools and techniques, is the foundational level. Using the tools (e.g., the principles of divergent and convergent thinking) correctly over time enhances one's cognitive and affective skills related to creativity. When these skills become integrated, people begin to use them naturally within and outside the workplace (e.g., in how they can help a neighbor, or in a discussion on world politics). As such they become a mindset, omnipresent, but unconsciously used. I deducted this approach from the leadership development model of Puccio, Mance, and Murdock (2011; see figure 1).

But there is a side note to be made in the context of self-managed organizations: whereas Puccio, Mance, and Murdock's (2011) model shows a learning path upwards, from creative tools to creative mindset, it is crucial for people interested in working in a self-managed organization to already possess a certain mindset in order to thrive in that kind of environment—even if they do not yet know the related creativity tools. I consider the most important mindsets to be a contribution mindset (Drucker, 2006), a learning mindset (Senge, 1990), and an internal locus of control (i.e., taking responsibility for one's own circumstances).

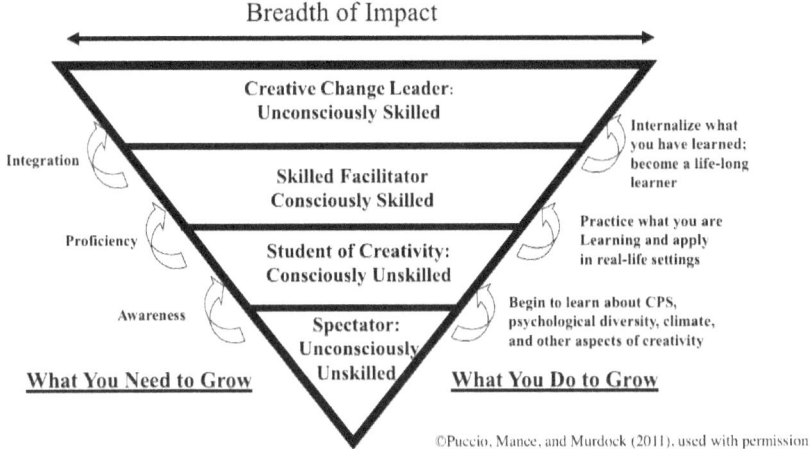

Figure 1: A model for the development of change leaders

Let us look more closely at some examples of how creativity can play a role in self-managed organizations, using the aforementioned layered approach.

How Can Creative Tools and Techniques Play a Role in Self-Managed Organizations?

In Decision Making

At GrantTree, workers needed to learn to make decisions more autonomously. Parnes (1967) taught us that creative behavior provides more effective decision making, followed by more intelligent action on decisions being taken:

> When a person makes creative decisions, he first speculates on what "might be" from a variety of viewpoints; then he senses and anticipates all conceivable consequences or repercussions and finally he chooses and develops his best alternative—in full awareness. (p. 6)

Knowing the steps in the Creative Problem Solving process (clarification, transformation, and implementation; Puccio, Mance, & Murdock, 2011), helps to structure your thinking process and ensures a well-balanced decision. When faced with a problem, the divergence-convergence balance will produce alternatives and prevent you from running with your first idea. Divergent thinking will also enable you to defer judgment when someone comes up with a different idea than you would have proposed.

In Meetings

A wide variety of topics are often discussed in team meetings. But, as many of you know, meetings can easily turn into nightmare situations. Self estimates of meeting productivity by managers in many different functional areas range from 33%-47% (Nicholas & Jay, 2001).

Learning creative tools to facilitate team meetings can prevent endless discussions and greatly enhance efficiency. This is what they have done at Buurtzorg, a Dutch neighborhood nursing company: all new recruits take a training course for healthy meetings and good decision-making. If teams get stuck despite their training, they can ask for an external facilitator (Laloux, 2014).

When Giving Feedback

There are no bosses, so providing feedback to your peers is crucial. Getting to know your and your colleagues' thinking profiles might provide a language to discuss differences and possible frictions. The FourSight Thinking Profile (Puccio, Miller, & Thurber, 2002) is an excellent instrument to provide that information as it measures your inborn preference for the phases in the problem solving process: clarify, ideate, develop and implement. When teams are composed, using the FourSight group profile can help clear up different roles and facilitate a discussion around the team's strengths and pitfalls (Puccio, Mance, & Murdock, 2011).

For Evaluation

At Gore, people are asked to rank their peers on the basis of who is making the biggest contribution to the success of the company, and whether they are behaving in collaborative ways and living the company values (Hamel, 2012). Evaluative tools such as card sort, paired comparison analysis and PPCo or POINt, among others, can certainly help to do so.

How Can a Creative Skill Set Play a Role in Self-Managed Organizations?

To illustrate this, I would like to expand upon the cognitive and affective skills in the Thinking Skills Model created by Puccio, Mance, and Murdock (2011; see Table 1).

Table 1: Thinking and Affective Skills in the Creative Problem Solving Thinking Skills Model

Step	Thinking Skill	Affective Skill
Assessing the situation	Diagnostic Thinking	Mindfulness
Exploring the Vision	Visionary Thinking	Dreaming
Formulating the Challenges	Strategic Thinking	Sensing gaps
Exploring Ideas	Ideational Thinking	Playfulness
Formulating Solutions	Evaluative Thinking	Avoiding premature closing
Exploring Acceptance	Contextual Thinking	Sensitivity to environment
Formulating a Plan	Tactical Thinking	Tolerance for risk

© Puccio, Mance, and Murdock (2011). Used with permission.

For each of the steps I will illustrate with an example how the skills can play a role in self-managed organizations.

The **over-arching skills** for a creative mindset are **openness for novelty** (being able to entertain ideas that at first seem outlandish and risky), **tolerance for complexity** (being able to stay open and persevere without being overwhelmed by large amounts of information, interrelated and complex issues, and competing perspectives), and **tolerance for ambiguity** (being able to deal with uncertainty and to avoid leaping to conclusions) (Puccio, Mance, & Murdock, 2011). When a company moves to self-management, everything is new and needs to be experimented with and thought out. Yes, there are books and previous cases to reference, but every company is different, so there is no such thing as a one size fits all approach. Thus, these three skills are not only over-arching in creativity, but also in self-management. Morning Star's Doug Kirkpatrick (2014) puts Tolerance for Ambiguity in his list of 5 crucial competences for self-management. Colman et al. (2015), CEO of Wit-Gele Kruis, stated, "Teaching people how to deal with ambiguity is crucial. Also, the board of directors and the coaches need to learn to live with the fact that they don't know everything and that that is ok" (p. 203).

The first step in the model is **Assessing the Situation** (to describe and identify relevant data and to determine the next step). The cognitive thinking skill used in this step is **Diagnostic Thinking** (making a careful examination of the situation, describing the challenge and deciding the appropriate steps), and the affective skill used is **Mindfulness** (attending to thoughts and feelings relative to the present situation; Puccio, Mance, & Murdock, 2011). These may prove to be the most essential skills, as assessing situations is critical to self-management. When employees are confronted with a problem, they will need to diagnose what is happening and come up with a proposal for a solution, as is illustrated by a nurse of Wit-Gele Kruis: "If we don't reach our financial targets, we are not happy. But we don't sit down and wait. Time for action! We think, make an analysis, evaluate several solutions and we take decisions" (Colman et al., 2015, p. 206). **Diagnostic Thinking** is crucial in order to know which step to take next.

The second step in the model is **Exploring the Vision** (to develop a vision of a desired outcome). The cognitive thinking skill used in this step is **Visionary Thinking** (articulating a vivid image of what you desire to create), and the affective skill used is **Dreaming** (to imagine as possible your desires and hopes) (Puccio, Mance, & Murdock, 2011). At Morning Star, the world's largest tomato processing company, there are no bosses: the mission is boss. Each employee is responsible for drawing up a personal mission statement that outlines how they will contribute to the company's goal (Hamel, 2012). This exercise demands visionary thinking and dreaming: not only should the employee have a clear vision of what he or she personally wants, the personal mission also needs to tie into the company's mission.The third step in the model is **Formulating Challenges** (to identify the gaps that must be closed to achieve the desired outcome). The cognitive skill that is used in this step is **Strategic Thinking** (identifying the critical issues that must be addressed and pathways needed to move toward the desired future), and the affective skill used is **Sensing Gaps** (to become consciously aware of the discrepancies between what currently exists and what is desired) (Puccio, Mance, & Murdock, 2011). In self-managed organizations, there are no bosses to tell you what to do; you need to keep an eye open for what needs to be done or what can be improved. The expression "Something needs to be done" is not tolerated (Laloux, 2014). The French brass factory FAVI is famous for its impeccable quality and trustworthiness. When due to a system glitch an order could not be delivered in time, workers self-organized, enlisted volunteers and added three shifts on Saturday and Sunday. Exhausted but proud, they got the job done, without management interference (Zobrist, 2007).

The fourth step in the model is **Exploring Ideas** (to generate novel ideas that address important challenges). The cognitive skill that is used is **Ideational Thinking** (producing original mental images and thoughts that respond to challenges), and the affective skill used is **Playfulness** (freely toying with ideas) (Puccio, Mance, & Murdock, 2011). In self-managed organizations, at least in the beginning of the self-managed structure, everything is new. At each step people have to ask themselves the question: "How is it done traditionally, and how else might I do it here?" They have to unlearn what they know and look at their work with an unprejudiced, child-like, vuja-dé mind (the opposite of déjà-vu; Kelley & Littman, 2005). At the Brazilian company Semco, an employee had an idea to reduce the manufacturing steps for a cutting machine. He didn't ask his boss, nor his colleagues, and set out to experiment. He succeeded and as a consequence, sales of the machine soared (Semler, 1993).

The fifth step in the model is **Formulating Solutions** (to move from ideas to solutions). The cognitive skill used is **Evaluative Thinking** (assessing the reasonableness and quality of ideas in order to develop workable solutions), and the affective skill in this step is **Avoiding Premature Closing** (resisting the urge to push for a decision) (Puccio, Mance, & Murdock, 2011). At Wit-Gele Kruis, teams reflect on their work at least once a year. They evaluate what has gone well, what needs improvement, and which resources they need (Colman et al., 2015). Formulating solutions is also necessary when people at Morning Star draw up their yearly CLOU (Colleague Letter of Understanding), a detailed description of how they will contribute to the mission, which activities they will perform, and what the metrics are (Hamel, 2012).

The sixth step in the model is **Exploring Acceptance** (to increase the likelihood of success). The cognitive skill associated with this step is **Contextual Thinking** (understanding the interrelated conditions that will support or hinder success) and its affective skill is **Sensitivity to Environment** (the degree to which people are aware of their physical and psychological surroundings) (Puccio, Mance, & Murdock, 2011). As there are no bosses to run to, a self-managed organization cannot function without excellent feedback. And although a combination of skills is needed for feedback, I want to highlight contextual thinking and sensitivity to environment. In order to provide helpful feedback, it is important to take the temperature of the situation and how the person opposite you perceives it, using your emotional and social intelligence. Adapting your communication (the what and the how) to that information will greatly enhance the result. At AES, Dennis Bakke got together with his closest peers once a year over dinner in one of their homes to share self-evaluations. They learned to comment, question and encourage each other to reach a deeper understanding of their potential and performance (Laloux, 2014).

The last step in the model is **Formulating a Plan** (to develop an implementation plan). The cognitive skill used is **Tactical Thinking** (devising a plan that includes specific and measurable steps for attaining a desired end and methods for monitoring its effectiveness). The affective skill in this step is **Tolerance for Risk** (not allowing yourself to be shaken or unnerved by the possibility of failure or setbacks) (Puccio, Mance, & Murdock, 2011). Taking initiative without instruction from your boss demands a certain tolerance for risk: you might make a mistake.

Asking your colleagues for advice can help, but ultimately, you're the one who decides. This is also a learning path for the leaders: they need to let people make mistakes. Bakke (2005) formulated it this way: "The most important part of our leadership style is letting others make the decisions" (p. 163).

How Can a Creative Mindset Play a Role?

Bakke (2005) stated:

> Behavior and virtues are not best learned through impersonal analysis of ethical choices or even intensive classroom training in right and wrong. For the most part we 'catch' character, virtue and values by practicing 'right' behaviors and actions so that they become first habits and then part of our character. (p. 160)

The same is said in creativity literature: once the tools and skills have been internalized, they become a set of active principles that transform behavior and attitudes in all aspects of one's life. Puccio, Mance, and Murdock (2011) believed that the greatest impact occurs at this level: "When creativity has been internalized, a person's behavior naturally begins to inspire creative change. Each interaction facilitates creative thinking in others" (p. 295).

At this stage, we might not have to ask ourselves where the link is between self-management & creativity: They have become one. In his book *Reinventing Organizations*, Laloux (2014) stated that the next stage of human consciousness, called Teal (elsewhere also referred to as integral), corresponds to Maslow's (1943) self-actualizing level. Rogers (1962) tied self-actualization to creativity, as he observed that the mainspring of creativity appeared to be the tendency to actualize oneself – the urge to expand, extend, develop and mature; the tendency to express and activate all of the capabilities of the organism. As such, one is no longer driven by external factors but by inner rightness: Does this decision seem right to me? With fewer ego-fears, we are able to make decisions that might seem risky, but that resonate with deep inner convictions, something essential in self-management (Laloux, 2014).

What About Leadership?

Enlightened leadership is essential in self-managed organizations. The most important character traits of a leader in this kind of organization are humility, the willingness to give up power, courage, integrity, and love and passion for the people, values, and mission of the organization (Bakke, 2005). Leaders of self-managing companies distribute their authority in the organization and take a more supportive role: Is the culture healthy? Are teams coming together? Are we getting diverse points of view? Those leaders have to be comfortable with not being at the center of all the action, not being behind every decision, and not being the most strategic person in the company (Hamel, 2012).

This description looks a lot like the one of transformational leadership, often associated with creative leadership. The transformative leader is attentive to the needs and motives of the followers and helps them reach their full potential. It is a two-way relationship, raising motivation and morality in both leader and followers (Northouse, 2016). That means that we also see a strong overlap between creativity and self-management in the field of leadership. Manz and Sims (2001) stated indeed that some of the strategies listed for what they call "SuperLeaders" (leading others to lead themselves) are conceptually similar to strategies recommended for supporting creativity, including the encouragement of learning from mistakes, sharing information, collaborating with others, and working interdependently. SuperLeaders promote creativity rather than conformity (Manz & Sims, 2001).

Conclusion and Recommendation

This paper demonstrates the role of creativity in self-managed organizations. Using many examples from concrete cases, I indicated in what ways creativity and creative leadership could be an answer, an added value, and even a necessity to these organizations' nature and needs. Self-management and creativity are strongly correlated, certainly in the higher levels. Even if these companies are already successful in their self-management practices, I am confident that learning or strengthening their knowledge of creative tools, skills, and mindsets, and being able to use the language for process, behavior, or leadership, will greatly enhance the quality of the collaboration in self-managed teams, and thus also the output. The importance of language cannot be emphasized enough, because the words we use have a powerful transformative influence on the way we think and act (Hurson, 2008).

My recommendation would be to introduce everyone in a self-managed company to creative thinking, to use it as part of the selection criteria for new hires, and to integrate it into the training programs. And of course, this method is not the purpose, as Chieh Tzu Yüan Hua Chuan so beautifully said: "Not to have a method is bad; to stop entirely at method is worse still. The aim of possessing method is to seem finally as if one had no method" (Hurson, 2008, p. 218).

References

Bakke, D. W. (2005). *Joy at work.* Seattle, WA: PVG.

Carney, B. M., & Getz, I. (2009). *Freedom, Inc.: Free your employees and let them lead your business to higher productivity, profits, and growth.* New York, NY: Crown Business.

Colman, K., de Caluwé, M., Dendooven, K., & van Landuyt, D. (2015). *De naakte waarheid over zelfsturing.* Tielt, Belgium: Lannoo Campus.

Drucker, P. F. (2006). *The effective executive: The definitive guide to getting the right things done.* New York, NY: HarperCollins.

Hamel, G. (2011, December). *First, let's fire all the managers.* Retrieved from https://hbr.org/2011/12/first-lets-fire-all-the-managers

Hamel, G. (2012). *What matters now: How to win in a world of relentless change, ferocious competition, and unstoppable innovation.* San Francisco, CA: Jossey-Bass.

Hamel, G. (2013, May). Leaders everywhere: A conversation with Gary Hamel (S. London, Interviewer). Retrieved from https://www.mckinsey.com/business-functions/organization/our-insights/leaders-everywhere-a-conversation-with-gary-hamel

Hurson, T. (2008). *Think better: An innovator's guide to productive thinking.* New York, NY: McGraw-Hill.

Kelley, T., & Littman, J. (2005). *The ten faces of innovation: IDEO's strategies for beating the devil's advocate & driving creativity throughout your organization.* New York, NY: Doubleday.

Kirkpatrick, D. (2014, April 17). *Five crucial competencies of self-management.* Retrieved from http://www.self-managementinstitute.org/five-crucial-competencies-of-self-management

Kniberg, H., & Ivarsson, A. (2012, October). *Scaling Agile @ Spotify with tribes, squads, chapters & guilds.* Retrieved from http://blog.crisp.se/wp-content/uploads/2012/11/SpotifyScaling.pdf

Laloux, F. (2014). *Reinventing organizations: A guide to creating organizations inspired by the next stage of human consciousness.* Brussels, Belgium: Nelson Parker.

Manz, C. C., & Sims, H. P. (2001). *The new superleadership: Leading others to lead themselves.* San-Francisco, CA: Berrett-Koehler.

Maslow, A. H. (1943). A theory of human motivation. *Psychological Review, 50*(4), 370-396.

Nicholas, C. R., & Jay, F. N. (2001). Meeting Analysis: Findings from Research and Practice. *Proceedings of the 34th Annual Hawaii International Conference on*. Maui, HI: System Sciences.

Northouse, P. G. (2016). *Leadership: Theory and practice* (7th ed.). Thousand Oaks, CA: SAGE Publications.

Parnes, S. J. (1967). *Creative behavior guidebook*. New York, NY: Charles Scribner's Sons.

Puccio, G. J., Mance, M., & Murdock, M. C. (2011). *Creative leadership: Skills that drive change* (2nd ed.). Thousand Oaks, CA: SAGE Publications.

Puccio, G. J. (with Miller, B, & Thurber, S). (2002). *FourSight – Your Thinking Profile: A tool for innovation*. Evanston, IL: THinc Communications.

Robertson, B. J. (2016). *Holacracy: The revolutionary management system that abolishes hierarchy*. New York, NY: Portfolio Penguin.

Rogers, C. (1962). Toward a theory of creativity. In S. J. Parnes & H. F. Harding (Eds.), *A source book for creative thinking* (pp. 65-66). New York, NY: Charles Scribner's Sons.

Semler, R. (1993). *Maverick: The success story behind the world's most unusual workplace*. New York, NY: Warner Books.

Senge, P. M. (1990). *The fifth discipline: The art & practice of the learning organization*. New York, NY: Currency.

Stichting Innovatie & Arbeid. (2014). *Knipperlicht voor burn-out*. Brussels, Belgium: Vlaamse Overheid.

Tenner, D. (2016, April 9). *An update on the advice process*. Retrieved from https://danieltenner.com/2016/04/09/an-update-on-the-advice-process/

Tenner, D. (2017, April 24). *Being teal vs being cool*. Retrieved from https://danieltenner.com/2017/04/24/being-teal-vs-being-cool/

Towers Watson. (2012). *Global workforce study: Engagement at risk: Driving strong performance in a volatile global environment*. Retrieved from http://employeeengagement.com/wp-content/uploads/2012/11/2012-Towers-Watson-Global-Workforce-Study.pdf

Zobrist, J.-F. (2007). *La belle histoire de Favi: L'Entreprise qui croit que l'Homme est bon*. Paris, France: Humanisme & Organisations.

About the Author

Ingrid De Clercq is co-founder of CONGAZ, an organization that specializes in "Tuning your Organization and People for Innovation". Noticing that companies often spend a lot of effort on the process-side of innovation, but a lot less on the human component, CONGAZ focuses on the people side of innovation, seeking to address the questions: How do you compose an innovative team? What is an innovative organization design? Which culture stimulates creativity? How do you deal with diversity?

Ingrid works on projects to realize culture change, building entrepreneurial teams, developing, launching and coaching innovation programs for larger companies, and building human resources in young, innovative companies. She lectures on team composition for entrepreneurial teams for Imperial College, London, the University of Brussels (VUB) and Erasmus College in Brussels. She has been a key note speaker and facilitator at innovation conferences in Belgium, Holland, France, Italy, Canada and Pakistan.

She is currently studying at the International Center for Studies in Creativity, of SUNY Buffalo State, and is a certified MBTI Trainer Type I & II, and a certified FourSight trainer.

e-mail: ingrid.declercq@congaz.be www.congaz.be
Linked in: https://www.linkedin.com/in/ingrid-de-clercq-a9562a/
Twitter: @ingriddeclercq

Is Female Leadership the Key to Unlocking Organizational Creativity?

Pamela Z. H. Pauwels
International Center for Studies in Creativity
SUNY Buffalo State

Abstract

Noland, Moran and Kotschwar (2016) found that having at least 30% female executives added 6% to a company's net profit margin when compared to similar firms with no women leaders. Sixty-one percent of 1500 executive leaders, interviewed by IBM, viewed creativity as an essential life skill in the increasingly complex world of business (IBM, 2010). While the body of research on the role of gender on business success is growing, research on organizational creativity and innovation has been characterized by gender blindness by not including gender as a research variable (Le Loarne-Lemaire & Gnan, 2015). This paper aims to answer the question, "Is female leadership the key to unlocking organizational creativity?" through exploring: 1) whether women are naturally more creative than men, as creative skills are required to lead creativity; 2) whether a female leadership style is more conducive to leading creativity; and 3) whether gender diversity leads to more organizational creativity. Despite the bias against female creative leaders (Cropley & Cropley, 2017), a case can be made that women hold the key to unlocking organizational creativity.

Is Female Leadership the Key to Unlocking Organizational Creativity?

Why are there "twice as many men called John as there are women leading FTSE100 companies" (Hosie, 2017, para. 1)? In the search to find an answer for the lack of women in executive and senior leadership roles, both scholars and practitioners have pondered over questions such as: 'Can women lead?' 'Are women better leaders?' and 'How do women effect overall (financial) results?' (Hoyt & Simon, 2016). Hoyt and Simon argued that although answers to these questions are often nuanced, contradictory, and dependent on varied factors, a trend is emerging which shows that having more women in senior leadership roles is beneficial to organizations. Hunt, Layton, and Prince (2015) found that companies with gender diversity were 15% more likely to outperform their peers. A recent study from the Peterson Institute for International Economics analyzed the financial results of nearly 22,000 global, publicly traded companies in 91 countries across different industries and sectors (Noland, Moran, & Kotschwar, 2016), and found that while the positive correlation between female CEOs and overall business results was not significant, having at least 30% female executives added 6% to a company's net profit margin when compared to similar firms with no women leaders. A meta-analysis carried out by Paustian-Underdahl, Walker, and Woehr (2014) showed no difference in perceived leadership effectiveness between men and women. However, when they excluded results that relied on self-ratings, women were perceived by others to be significantly more effective than men and were also seen as better leaders in business and educational organizations. A study carried by Zenger and Folkman (2012) found that women rated higher than men in 12 of the 16 competencies measured related to outstanding leadership. On two traits which have historically not been attributed to women, "taking initiative" and "driving for results", women outscored men to the highest degree (Zenger & Folkman, 2012). After conducting a study among 2,900 Norwegian leaders, the BI Norwegian Business School researchers concluded that when it comes to personality traits such as clarity, innovation, support, and targeted meticulousness, females are better suited for leadership than their male colleagues (Martinsen & Glasø, 2013).

These analects reflect two common arguments found in the literature on why women deserve more executive leadership positions. The first is the personality- or trait-driven argument, which shows a direct link between gender and business results by arguing that certain female characteristics make women better leaders than men. The second, the diversity argument, does not necessarily favor one gender above the other and sees a more indirect link between women leaders and business results by arguing that gender diversity leads to better business outcomes.

While business results are imperative for the long-term survival of an organization, they are not all that matters. In a study carried out by IBM among 1,600 CEOs, business leaders agreed that to deal with increasing complexity in the world and in business, creativity must be instilled throughout the organization (2010). If more senior female leaders lead to better business results, would this also translate into increased organizational creativity? Is the lack of female leaders in senior positions holding organizations back on creativity and innovation? Could female leadership hold the key to unlocking creative potential?

Leadership, Organizational Creativity, and Gender

Dawson & Andriopoulos (2014) stated that leadership plays a crucial role in change, creativity, and innovation. Puccio and Cabra (2010) argued that leadership is probably one of the most salient elements of a work environment in promoting creativity. Through their behaviors, abilities, and qualities, leaders can encourage an environment that leads to creativity and innovation (both of which will henceforth be referred to interchangeably, as all innovation relies on creative thought). Although a clearer picture is emerging around the link between leadership and organizational creativity, very little attention has been given so far to the role that gender might play. When looking at the field of innovation, gender and innovation are rarely explored together. Hunter, Bedell, and Mumford (2007) argued that researching gender issues is complicated due the lack of systematic studies and use of mixed samples. Le Loarne-Lemaire and Gnan (2015) found that innovation literature and research have been characterized by gender blindness by not including gender as a research variable.

Due to this lack of research, the question of whether female leadership holds the key to unlocking creative potential in businesses needs to be answered indirectly. To realize innovation and creative success, a leader must have relevant creative abilities (Ruiz-Jiménez & del Mar Fuentes-Fuentes, 2016) and possess adequate skills in terms of creative problem solving (e.g. Mumford, Connelly, & Gaddis, 2003; Tierney, 2008). Based on these statements, there are three potential routes to validate or refute the hypothesis that women are better creative leaders. First, one could argue that if women are more creative by nature, they should be better creative leaders. Second, women seem to enhance organizational creativity through inherent female characteristics or traits that may be more conducive for leading creativity. And finally, having more female leaders contributes to diversity of thought, and therefore might lead to more organizational creativity.

Are Females More Creative Than Males?

During the 1950s, Alex Osborn (1953) tried to answer the question on gender differences in creativity in his book, *Applied Imagination*. Ultimately, he found that research on gender and creativity was inconclusive. While, in some studies, women demonstrated more imagination and creativity (Osborn, 1953), other research did not find any significant difference in creativity by gender (Milton, 1957; Torrance, 1959). Over 60 years later, Stoltzfus, Nibbelink, Vredenburg, and Thyrum (2011) observed that no clear picture has emerged on the relationship between gender and creativity. Baer and Kaufman (2008) concluded in a literature review on creativity and gender that although there were differences in patterns and areas of strengths between the genders, there was relative equality in creative ability. In a recent overview of psychological and neuroscientific literature, Abraham (2016) concluded:

> In bringing together diverse bodies of evidence that have explored gender differences in cognition and brain function, the take-home message from this overview is that the sexes do not differ in terms of global or specific intellectual abilities but may do so in the cognitive strategies, functional task sets or cognitive styles that each are physiologically predisposed to adopt. (p. 615)

Overall, the literature paints a complex picture on whether one gender is naturally more predisposed to be creative than the other. Therefore, the conclusion cannot be made that women are better creative leaders because they are more creative by nature than men. Acknowledging that there are differences between women and men in terms of expressing creativity and cognitive strategies might influence how females lead others in terms of creativity.

Are Female Personalities Better Suited for Creative Leadership?

When it comes to leadership, women are often under different pressures than men. Like their male counterparts, female leaders need to live up to expectations and be competent, but they are also expected to emphasize their femininity. Therefore, a transformational leadership style that would be beneficial for women would link traditional female characteristics such as consideration, empowerment, and support to leadership effectiveness (Hoyt & Simon, 2016). Wolfram and Gratton (2014) found that for female managers, when adopting a transformational leadership style, displaying typical gender attributes was positively related to charisma and inspiration. A transformational leadership style is not only linked to female leadership, but to creative leadership in general, due to the focus on change and the reciprocity between leaders and followers, which leads both to higher levels of motivation and morality (Puccio, Mance, & Murdock, 2011). Carmeli, Sheaffer, Binyamin, Reiter-Palmon, and Shimoni (2014) found that transformational leaders play an influential role in nurturing the creative problem solving capacities of their followers by facilitating a perception of psychological safety and reflexivity processes. According to Carmeli et al. (2014), "transformational leaders are attuned to individuals, create a shared vision, act as role models, and encourage followers to go beyond their current needs and expectations and realize their creative potential as it pertains to solving ill-defined problems creatively" (pp. 129-130). Through a transformational leadership style, women might be more adept at enhancing creativity. Reiter-Palmon and Illies (2004) argued that the leader's role in facilitating creativity might be in creating a culture that allows ideas to be exchanged openly, and where there is mutual trust among the group members and between the group members and the leader. Studies have shown that women tend to score higher than men on traits like openness and support (Martinsen, 2014; Martinsen & Glasø, 2013; Zenger & Folkman, 2012). Post (2015) further found that women leaders were better at creating cohesion among large and functionally-diverse teams and stimulating cooperative learning and participative communication on larger and geographically dispersed teams. All of this suggests that women might be better at supporting a climate for creativity than men. A case can easily be made that female leaders are better equipped to enhance creative potential in organizations, as the general female leadership style and personality is more beneficial in unlocking organizational creativity than its male counterpart. However, more research is needed to fully understand the link between gender, leadership, and creative achievement, as only a handful of creative leadership studies currently include gender as a variable, since most studies are based on mixed samples and control for gender effects.

Does Gender Diversity Lead to More Organizational Creativity?

The evidence is stacking up that gender diversity has a favorable influence on creativity and innovation. Østergaard, Timmermans, and Kristinsson (2011) found that when it comes to being creative, groups benefit from many areas of diversity, including the group's gender composition. The authors further showed that following educational diversity, gender diversity has the strongest correlation with an organization's likelihood to innovate, though this impact is somewhat overlooked in the innovation literature (Østergaard et al., 2011). Ruiz-Jiménez and del Mar Fuentes-Fuentes (2016) studied the role of women on the boards of technology-based small and medium-sized enterprises, and their impact on management capabilities and innovation. They found that "management capabilities have a greater influence on both product and process innovation when the management team is more balanced in the number of men and women" (Ruiz-Jiménez & del Mar Fuentes-Fuentes, 2016, p. 107). The authors concluded that:

> Gender diversity in the top management team thus seems to encourage a work climate that stimulates development of innovative ideas, exchange of knowledge, communication, and trust, while also favoring execution of more processes and routines, and use of resources that are more effective in achieving innovation in products and processes. (Ruiz-Jiménez & del Mar Fuentes-Fuentes, 2016, p. 118)

However, merely adding women to leadership roles might not be enough. The number of women within those roles also matters. Torchia, Calabrò, and Huse (2011) found that a firm needed to add three or more women to its board to enhance its level of innovativeness. Yet Cropley and Cropley (2017) argued that organizations seeking to improve their innovation capacity must do more than simply increase gender diversity. There must be an alignment between gender diversity and the organizational culture. For example, in cultures that favor more masculine characteristics—e.g. competition or thirst for power—over more feminine characteristics—e.g. personal, social, entrusting, contributory, collaborative, or vicarious—the contribution of women is likely to be inhibited or blocked, even if these women are perceived to have a masculine achieving style. It is clear that gender diversity and adding more female leaders to management roles should increase organizational creativity. Therefore, could the fact that the literature on creativity, innovation, and leadership is mainly gender blind instill a bias against women when it comes to creative leadership?

Is There a Bias Against Female Creative Leaders?

Based on the research, it appears that a case can be made for including more women in leadership roles to achieve greater success in businesses' innovation processes. So why are female creative leaders still in the minority? For example, in the United States, less than 20% of patents include at least one-woman inventor (Quinn, 2016). Stereotypes towards female leadership, creativity, and innovation are tenacious. Cropley and Cropley (2015; 2017) observed that male stereotypes, such as risk seeking and driving for results, are perceived by organizations to be more innovative than female stereotypes, such as being more orientated to people, process, culture, and front-end idea generation. Although the latter are key to creativity (Rhodes, 1961), somehow, they seem to be perceived as a hindrance to innovative behavior in organizations. In a series of experiments, Proudfoot, Kay, and Koval (2015) found that men's ideas were seen as more creative, even when women produced identical outcomes. Female executives were also stereotyped as being less creative than their male counterparts when evaluated by their supervisors, but not by their direct reports.

As previously explored, the organizational culture can have a strong effect on the creative potential of women. Foss, Woll, and Moilanen (2013) considered the innovation processes, as all organizational processes, to be highly gendered: anything masculine is typically credited with a higher value than what is considered feminine. The authors found that innovations stemming from women's idea generation were largely unexploited, and women's ideas were less frequently implemented than those of men (Foss, Woll, & Moilanen, 2013). Okon-Horodynska, and Zachorowska-Mazurkiewicz (2015) argued:

> The essence of the research is that, while men and women are equally innovative, their gender role within the context of an organization can affect how they are perceived and how they behave when innovating and sharing ideas. Men are perceived as more innovative and risk-taking, and women are perceived as more adaptive and risk adverse. Thus, gender roles may interact with the role of the manager to inhibit (in the case of women) or facilitate (in the case of men) the likelihood of innovative behavior. (p. 12)

Although women and men might be equal in creative potential, the bias against female creative leadership is strong. Organizations who are seeking to enhance their creative potential by including more women in their senior ranks will have to pay attention and put forth effort to neutralize the tangible and intangible causes of bias against female creative leaders.

Gender and Creative Leadership: Concluding Thoughts

This paper aimed to answer the question, "Is female leadership the key to unlocking organizational creativity?" While it might be somewhat narrow-minded to blatantly attribute male and female characteristics to their respective genders, as these characteristics are "notoriously changeable" (Pecis, 2016, p. 2123) and are constantly redefined in relation to each other, the sad truth is that while males and females bring the same innate capacity for innovation to organizations, innovation remains a 'men's business' (Cropley & Cropley, 2017). This is an enormous waste of talent in an era where creativity and innovation are recognized as necessary for organizational adaptation and survival (Reiter-Palmon, 2011). Unlocking organizational creativity is a complex phenomenon requiring focus on both individual and organizational factors (Robinson-Morral, Reiter-Palmon,

& Kaufman, 2013). Both genders, as creative leaders, need to understand their own strengths and weaknesses, and how these facilitate or inhibit creativity and innovation within their organizations (Hunter, Thoroughgood, Myer, & Ligon 2011). This might not be enough, however, as organizations may require the establishment of policies and procedures to create a climate of inclusion that harnesses the diversity of innovation, effectiveness, and well-being (Guillaume et al., 2014). Keeping the above in mind, the question can be answered affirmatively. Due to their transformational leadership styles and their positive influences on gender diversity, female leaders hold the key to (further) unlocking organizational creativity. As the Polish saying goes: "Where the devil does not manage, it sends a woman" (Okon-Horodynska & Zachorowska-Mazurkiewicz, 2015, p. 10).

References

Abraham, A. (2016). Gender and creativity: An overview of psychological and neuroscientific literature. *Brain Imaging and Behavior, 10*(2), 609-618. doi: 10.1007/s11682-015-9410-8

Baer, J., & Kaufman, J. C. (2008). Gender differences in creativity. *The Journal of Creative Behavior, 42*(2), 75-105. doi: 10.1002/j.2162-6057.2008.tb01289

Carmeli, A., Sheaffer, Z., Binyamin, G., Reiter-Palmon, R., & Shimoni, T. (2014). Transformational leadership and creative problem-solving: The mediating role of psychological safety and reflexivity. *The Journal of Creative Behavior, 48*(2), 115-135. doi: 10.1002/jocb.43

Cropley, D. H., & Cropley, A. J. (2015). *The psychology of innovation in organizations*. New York, NY: Cambridge University Press.

Cropley, D. H., & Cropley, A. (2017). Innovation capacity, organisational culture and gender. *European Journal of Innovation Management, 20*(3), 493-510. doi: 10.1108/EJIM-12-2016-0120

Dawson, P., & Andriopoulos, C. (2014). *Managing change, creativity & innovation* (2nd ed.). Thousand Oaks, CA: SAGE Publications.

Foss, L., Woll, K., & Moilanen, M. (2013). Creativity and implementations of new ideas: Do organisational structure, work environment and gender matter? *International Journal of Gender and Entrepreneurship, 5*(3), 298-322. doi: 10.1108/IJGE-09-2012-0049

Guillaume, Y. R. F., Dawson, J. F., Priola, V., Sacramento, C. A., Woods, S. A., Higson, H. E., ... West, M. A. (2014). Managing diversity in organizations: An integrative model and agenda for future research. *European Journal of Work and Organizational Psychology, 23*(5), 783-802. doi: 10.1080/1359432X.2013.805485

Hosie, R. (2017, March 30). *Women are better leaders than men, study of 3,000 managers concludes.* Retrieved from http://www.independent.co.uk/lifestyle/women-better-leaders-men-study-a7658781.html

Hoyt, C. L. & Simon, S. (2016). Gender and leadership. In P. G. Northouse (Ed,) *Leadership: Theory and practice* (7th ed.) (pp. 397-426). Los Angeles, CA: SAGE Publications.

Hunt, V., Layton, D., & Prince, S. (2015, January). *Why diversity matters.* Retrieved from http://www.mckinsey.com/business-functions/organization/

Hunter, S. T., Bedell, K. E., & Mumford, M. D. (2007). Climate for creativity: A quantitative review. *Creativity Research Journal, 19*(1), 69-90. doi: 10.1080/10400410709336883

Hunter, S. T., Thoroughgood, C. N., Myer, A. T., & Ligon, G. S. (2011). Paradoxes of leading innovative endeavors: Summary, solutions, and future directions. *Psychology of Aesthetics, Creativity, and the Arts, 5*(1), 54-66.

IBM. (2010, May 18). *IBM 2010 Global CEO Study: Creativity selected as most crucial factor for future success.* Retrieved from https://www-03.ibm.com/press/us/en/pressrelease/31670.wss

Le Loarne-Lemaire, S., & Gnan, L. (2015). Is innovation gendered? *International Journal of Entrepreneurship and Small Business, 24*(1), 1-3.

Martinsen, Ø., & Glasø, L (2013). Personality and management. In R. Rønning, W. Brochs- Haukedal, L. Glasø, & S. B. Matthiesen (Eds.), *Life as a leader. Leather Study 3.0* (pp. 47-72). Bergen, Norway: Fagbokforlaget.

Milton, G. A. (1957). The effects of sex-role identification upon problem-solving skill. *The Journal of Abnormal and Social Psychology, 55*(2), 208-212.

Mumford, M. D., Connelly, S., & Gaddis, B. (2003). How creative leaders think: Experimental findings and cases. *The Leadership Quarterly, 14*(4), 411-432. doi: 10.1016/S1048-9843(03)00045-6

Noland, M., Moran, T., & Kotschwar, B. (2016, February). Is gender diversity profitable? Evidence from a global survey. *Working Paper Series, 16-3.* Retrieved from https://piie.com/publications/working-papers/gender-diversity-profitable-evidence-global-survey

Northouse, P. G. (2016). *Leadership: Theory and practice* (7th Ed.). Los Angeles, CA: SAGE Publications.

Okon-Horodynska, E., & Zachorowska-Mazurkiewicz, A. (2015). Innovation, innovativeness and gender: Approaching innovative gender. *Scientific Annals of the "Alexandru Ioan Cuza" University of Iasi Economic Sciences, 62*(1), 1-22. doi: 10.1515/aicue-2015-0001

Osborn, A. F. (1953). Applied imagination: Principles and procedures of creative problem-solving. New York, NY: Scribner.

Østergaard, C. R., Timmermans, B., & Kristinsson, K. (2011). Does a different view create something new? The effect of employee diversity on innovation. *Research Policy, 40*(3), 500-509. doi: 10.1016/j.respol.2010.11.004

Paustian-Underdahl, S. C., Walker, L. S., & Woehr, D. J. (2014). Gender and perceptions of leadership effectiveness: A meta-analysis of contextual moderators. *Journal of Applied Psychology, 99*(6), 1129-1145.

Pecis, L. (2016). Doing and undoing gender in innovation: Femininities and masculinities in innovation processes. *Human Relations, 69*(11), 2117-2140. doi: 10.1177/0018726716634445

Post, C. (2015). When is female leadership an advantage? Coordination requirements, team cohesion, and team interaction norms. *Journal of Organizational Behavior, 36*(8), 1153-1175. doi: 10.1002/job.2031

Proudfoot, D., Kay, A. C., & Koval, C. Z. (2015). A gender bias in the attribution of creativity: Archival and experimental evidence for the perceived association between masculinity and creative thinking. *Psychological Science, 26*(11), 1751-1761. doi: 10.1177/0956797615598739

Puccio, G. J., & Cabra, J. F. (2010). Organizational creativity: A systems approach. In J. C. Kaufman & R. J. Sternberg (Eds), *The Cambridge handbook of creativity* (pp. 145-173). New York, NY: Cambridge University Press.

Puccio, G. J., Mance, M., & Murdock, M. (2011). *Creative leadership: Skills that drive change* (2nd ed.). Thousand Oaks, CA: SAGE Publications.

Quinn, G. (2016, August 1). The patent gender gap: Less than 20% of U.S. patents have at least one woman inventor. Retrieved from http://www.ipwatchdog.com

Reiter-Palmon, R. (2011). Introduction to special issue: The psychology of creativity and innovation in the workplace. *Psychology of Aesthetics, Creativity, and the Arts, 5*(1), 1-2. doi: 10.1037/a0018586

Reiter-Palmon, R., & Illies, J. J. (2004). Leadership and creativity: Understanding leadership from a creative problem-solving perspective. *The Leadership Quarterly, 15*(1), 55-77. doi: 10.1016/j.leaqua.2003.12.005

Rhodes, M. (1961). An analysis of creativity. *The Phi Delta Kappan, 42*(7), 305-310.

Robinson-Morral, E. J., Reiter-Palmon, R., & Kaufman, J. C. (2013). The interactive effects of self-perceptions and job requirements on creative problem solving. *The Journal of Creative Behavior, 47*(3), 200-214.

Ruiz-Jiménez, J. M., & del Mar Fuentes-Fuentes, M. (2016). Management capabilities, innovation, and gender diversity in the top management team: An empirical analysis in technology-based SMEs. *BRQ Business Research Quarterly, 19*(2), 107-121. doi: 10.1016/j.brq.2015.08.003

Stoltzfus, G., Nibbelink, B. L., Vredenburg, D., & Thyrum, E. (2011). Gender, gender role, and creativity. *Social Behavior and Personality: An InternationalJjournal, 39*(3), 425-432. doi: 10.2224/sbp.2011.39.3.425

Tierney, P. (2008). Leadership and employee creativity. In J. Zhou & C. E. Shalley (Eds.), *Handbook of organizational creativity* (pp. 95-124). New York, NY: Lawrence Erlbaum Associates.

Torchia, M., Calabrò, A., & Huse, M. (2011). Women directors on corporate boards: From tokenism to critical mass. *Journal of Business Ethics, 102*(2), 299-317. doi: 10.1007/s10551-011-0815-z

Torrance, E. P. (1959). *Sex-role identification and creative thinking*. Minneapolis, MN: Bureau of Educational Research, University of Minnesota.

Wolfram, H.-J., & Gratton, L. (2014). Gender role self-concept, categorical gender, and transactional-transformational leadership: Implications for perceived workgroup performance. *Journal of Leadership & Organizational Studies, 21*(4), 338-353. doi: 10.1177/1548051813498421

Zenger, J., & Folkman J. (2012, March 15). *Are women better leaders than men?* Retrieved from https://hbr.org/2012/03/a-study-in-leadership-women-do

About the Author

Pamela Pauwels (PhD) is a Market Segment Leader at Eastman Chemical B.V. (NL) and heads the European marketing team for the Specialty Plastics business. Over the years she has led and coached many multidisciplinary innovation teams at Eastman, Philips and Unilever. Fascinated by the field of creativity and innovation, she was looking for further inspiration, theoretical frameworks and more efficient tools. This sparked her to pursue her Master in Creativity and Change Leadership from the International Center from Studies in Creativity at SUNY Buffalo State (NY), which she gained in 2017. Pamela previously studied Psychology at the Catholic University Leuven (Belgium) (1991) and holds a PhD in Psychology from the University of Exeter (UK) (1997) (focus: risk perception and decision-making).

Email: pamela.pauwels@xs4all.nl
LinkedIn: http://www.linkedin.com/pub/pamela-pauwels/2/800/51b

Why Do Nonprofits Need Creativity and How Might Creativity Differ in Nonprofit Organizations?

Alice F. Jacobs
International Center for Studies in Creativity
SUNY Buffalo State

Abstract

Nonprofit organizations are in large part responsible for how we preserve and further our culture, and how we, as human beings, care for each other. Their influence is felt in every area of modern society: health and wellbeing, the environment, culture, and education. In today's fast-changing world, more than ever, organizations dealing with social and cultural issues need to be at the forefront of creative work—to imagine the challenges we may face and the opportunities that may arise in the next century. Research into the process of creativity and innovation in the nonprofit environment is called for as there is sufficient empirical and anecdotal evidence to conclude that, while the cognitive processes of creativity may not differ, the influencing factors and mechanisms that contribute to the process do. This paper discusses how the creativity and innovation process of nonprofits may be the same and may differ from for–profit organizations.

The Case for Creativity in Nonprofit Organizations

Nonprofit organizations are in large part responsible for how we preserve and further our culture, and how we, as human beings, care for each other. Many fields, such as those focusing on health and wellbeing, the environment, culture, and education, have experienced their benefits. Nonprofit organizations aspire to be transformational to our society, driving social change in specific areas, thus working to create vibrant, just communities; the type of communities that attract the talent of the next generation. In this way, nonprofit organizations are essential to the future vitality and prosperity of our communities.

To truly transform society, we are faced with a need to resolve increasingly complex social issues. These issues can be characterized as novel and unique, lacking definition as to exactly what the issue is and uncertainty as to what information might be relevant for potential solutions. Clean drinking water, gender pay inequity, inner-city high school graduation rates, and sustainable food sources are a few examples of these issues. Everywhere you look, there are critical issues and opportunities that nonprofits are tackling. Camillus (2008) and Rittel and Webber (1973) referred to these issues as 'wicked problems' which are characterized as follows:

> (1) the issue's roots are complex and tangled; (2) the problem is difficult to come to grips with and changes; (3) every wicked problem is essentially unique; (4) there's nothing to indicate the right answer to the problem; (5) the problem involves many stakeholders with different values and priorities; (6) the causes...can be described in numerous ways; and (7) every wicked problem can be considered the symptoms of another problem. (Puccio, Mance & Murdock, 2011, pp. 65-66)

What does it take to build inroads into these intractable problems – to create opportunity where for a long time we have seen a lack of progress? Two innovative programs within my own community demonstrate some of the variables that make a difference. The first is *Say Yes to Education Buffalo* (n.d.), a partnership initiative that created a collaboration between school districts; parents; teachers; administrators; state, city and county governments; higher education; community-based organizations; businesses; and foundations. The purpose of this initiative is to increase high school and postsecondary completion rates in the city of Buffalo, New York. By connecting the economic vitality of the region and the need to sustain and build the city population with college scholarships for all those who graduate, the program incentivized the districts, teachers, families, and students to embrace change. Over a five- year period, the high school graduation rate in the city of Buffalo increased 12%, and postsecondary enrollment increased 10%.

Second, the *MOMS: From Education to Employment* initiative of the WNY Women's Foundation (n.d.) chose to focus specifically on the target population of single mothers who had attempted college previously and dropped out. By listening to these single mothers and designing the initiative around their perspective, over the course of a three-year collaboration with Niagara County Community College, the program helped 255 mothers complete a degree, and increased the retention rate for single moms to almost 100%. This program also influenced over 400 children who now see their mothers as role models for education. What has enabled these initiatives to succeed where many others have tried and failed? From my perspective, I see the differentiating factor as creativity: the willingness of the stakeholders to think differently, take risks, and connect people, ideas, and resources in pursuit of innovative solutions.

How do we unleash this creative potential in other nonprofit organizations? The complexity of the issues and opportunities faced, and the herculean task of delivering on ambitious missions with limited resources, call for nonprofit organizations to engage in visionary and creative thinking to find innovative solutions. And yet, Morris, Coombes, Allen, and Schindehutte (2007) believed that "the logic of engaging in innovative, risk-taking behaviors while also attempting to serve a social mission... and satisfy multiple stakeholders typically with severely limited resources, is not always clear cut" (Coombes, Morris, Allen, & Webb, 2011, p. 829). There is limited research focused on understanding what drives creativity and how the process might differ in the nonprofit environment from that of for-profit entities. An understanding of this complex process, and of how to encourage creativity *that leads to innovation* in organizations working to better our world, for the future will serve us all.

What Does Innovation Mean in Nonprofit Organizations?

Answering the threshold question, "What does innovation mean in nonprofit organizations?" is fundamental to understanding how the process of creativity might vary from the for-profit business environment. The relatively new concept of social innovation appears to encompass the highest level of innovation a nonprofit organization would strive to achieve. Mumford (2002) defined social innovation as "the generation and implementation of new ideas about how people should organize interpersonal activities, or social interactions, to meet one or more common goals" (p. 253). Mumford's definition conceives of social innovation as a continuum, with some innovations rising to the level of a new kind of institution and others being at the level of a new avenue for collaborative work. Examples on the continuum range from the achievements of Martin Luther and Karl Marx to the creation of the Boy Scouts and the implementation of flexible work schedules. Phills, Deiglmeier, and Miller (2008) provided another useful definition of social innovation: "a novel solution to a social problem that is more effective, efficient, sustainable or just than existing solutions and for which the value created accrues primarily to society as a whole rather than private individuals" (p. 36).

Another relevant concept to consider is social entrepreneurship; those who create social innovations are sometimes referred to as social entrepreneurs (Gunn & Durkin, 2010; Jiang & Thagard, 2014). Building on Brooks' (2008) research, Coombes et al. (2011) defined social entrepreneurship as being "concerned with the pursuit of opportunities for enhancing social good, where unique resource combinations are used to produce significant social returns" (p. 829). Examples of entrepreneurial behavior in nonprofits include expanding services, generating new and diversified revenue sources, pursuing partnerships and mergers, implementing innovative approaches to operations, and developing and using evaluation methods to measure social returns on program investments. The commonalities in these examples are the associated innovative, proactive, and risk-taking behaviors that led to their implementations, as well their positive impacts on organizational sustainability and mission fulfillment (Coombes et al., 2011).

Whether by achieving a true social innovation, an iterative improvement on a process impacting the community, or a change leading to future sustainability or increased relevance for an organization, innovation is taking place. Understanding the processes and influences that have driven these instances may shed light on the mechanisms that foster the creative process in nonprofit organizations.

Is the Process of Creativity Different in Social Innovation?

Not all creative acts in nonprofit organizations can or should rise to the level of social innovation to create meaningful change and improve on mission delivery. However, it is helpful to examine the limited existing research on creative processes leading to social innovation to address the question: Are there significant differences in the creative process in the nonprofit context?

Jiang and Thagard (2014) conducted case studies of the cognitive process involved in six cases of social innovation, including the development of Teach for America, Habitat for Humanity, and microfinance initiatives. Their findings supported their hypotheses, which aligned social innovation with creativity in problem solving in other domains: "Generally, the process of social innovation starts with goals that initiate intentional problem solving that leads to solutions by means of reasoning, association, analogy and conceptual combinations" (Jiang & Thagard, 2014, p. 383). Although the authors concluded that creativity in social innovation was largely aligned with creativity in other domains, they found that two elements differed: 1) social innovation draws direct inspiration from visual and verbal connections with those on whose lives the innovation is focused, meaning that empathy is a greater motivational factor than in other domains of creativity; and 2) social innovation plays off social mechanisms of emotions, such as mimicry and sympathy, that are reactions to the condition of others, while typically the creative process is driven more by an individual's internally-generated emotions (Jiang & Thagard, 2014). These two factors do not seem to be significant enough to support a conclusion that the process of creativity leading to innovation in nonprofit organizations differs from other domains, although the motivational factors may vary in influence.

Although research has suggested that social innovation is not a separate innovation class, one unique aspect of social innovation that may imply some difference in problem solving approaches is that social innovation often focuses on "procedural creativity, where the new product is a method consisting of new rules for doing things" (Jiang & Thagard, 2014, p. 376). Procedural creativity is present when social innovation is defined as a "means to an end rather than an anticipated outcome of a given process" (Grimm, Fox, Baines, & Albertson, 2013, p. 438). This difference raises the question for investigation as to whether creative process differs when the end goal for an innovation is not articulated as a product or service.

How Might Various Factors Influencing Creativity Operate in the Nonprofit Context?

If the process underlying creativity in nonprofits is essentially the same as in other domains, the question remains of how various influencing factors may operate in the nonprofit environment to enable organizations to harness the power of creativity. Without a profit motive, what drives the organizational culture to encourage creative thinking leading to innovation? How might the many complex factors influencing creativity and innovation play out differently? There are a few factors that I believe particularly merit further examination: leadership influence, cultural influences, and motivational influences.

Leadership Influence. Studies support the theory that leadership significantly impacts creativity and innovation in an organization (Puccio et al., 2011). To understand creativity and innovation in nonprofits, we need to discern whether leadership plays the same role with respect to fostering creativity as in other organizations. The beginnings of a body of research are developing around this issue: Allen, Smith, and Da Silva (2013), investigated the impact of leadership on a nonprofit church's organizational climate and found a positive correlation between a transformational leadership style and the organization's level of change readiness and willingness to accept creative ideas. This finding suggests that nonprofit leaders should pay heed to a focus on effective leadership style in encouraging creativity and innovation within their organizations. Jaskyte's (2004) study of nonprofit human services organizations found no correlation between transformational leadership and organizational innovativeness, but did find a positive relationship between a number of transformational leadership practices and cultural consensus. Cultural consensus, demonstrating the degree to which members share common values, was shown in this study to be negatively related to innovation (Jaskyte, 2004), implying that the values underlying the cultural consensus in the subject organizations may have been contrary to encouraging creativity and innovation. Jaskyte's (2004) findings suggest that nonprofit leaders need to focus on the organizational culture and the values it reflects, working to ensure that the culture incorporates values that have been demonstrated to foster innovation. This implication is consistent with findings of other studies based on for-profit entities (Isaksen & Akkermans, 2011).

Although in some respects the influence of nonprofit leadership to encourage creativity and innovation may align with that of other types of organizations, understanding its impact is challenged by the complexity of leadership structures in typical organizations. Unlike for-profit entities, the influence of the nonprofit Board of Directors is combined with the CEO or Executive Director in establishing the organizational culture (Coombes et al., 2011). Coombes and colleagues (2011) found a significant connection between a nonprofit board's behavioral dimensions and the entrepreneurial orientation of the organization. This orientation impacts the propensity and ability of the organization to "innovate, take risks and be proactive" (Coombes et al., 2011, p. 848). The implications of this study are that a board may inhibit or enhance creativity and innovation in the organization it serves. For leadership, this means that both employed and volunteer leadership personnel in nonprofits must be skilled and motivated to lead, so as to foster creativity.

I have found scarce resources on the mechanisms through which a nonprofit board may influence an organization's culture for innovation. Jaskyte (2012) proposed a model demonstrating how board structures and processes may influence the ability of a nonprofit to innovate. The model sets forth direct and indirect factors, including board capital (inclusive of intellectual resources), board culture and cohesiveness, and relationships between the executive director and the board chair (Jaskyte, 2012). Coombes et al. (2011) envisioned a board as capable of filling an essential role as a strategic resource for nonprofits, to understand and act on the need for change and innovation, and they acknowledged the need to establish an operational model to understand how this impact might best be achieved. Chait, Ryan, and Taylor (2005) advocated for boards to engage in "generative thinking" (p. 99), citing three factors that give boards a unique position: power—stemming from the board's loci of legitimacy and authority; plurality—the rich mix of perceptions, knowledge, and insights that result from a board's diversity; and positioning—the unique perspective of being closely connected yet at enough distance to step back and see the larger picture. The concept of generative thinking incorporates problem and opportunity sensing that enables "a new sense of things...a new perspective...a 'paradigm shift'" (Chait et al., 2005, pp. 79-80). While Chait et al. (2005) set forth insightful, practical tactics for engaging a board in generative thinking, the work needs to be expanded to demonstrate how these practices relate to organizational innovation.

Cultural Influences. We should also consider whether the values that traditionally hold sway in nonprofit cultures might be stumbling blocks for nonprofit leaders in orienting their cultures to encourage innovation. In Jaskyte's (2004) study on transformational leadership and nonprofit organizations, the values primarily reflected in the cultural consensus were stability, teamwork, detail orientation, and people orientation. *Challenging the Process,* the only transformational leadership practice not correlated with the cultural consensus in the study, encompasses leadership acts that foster behavior supporting innovation, such as challenging the status quo, experimenting with new ideas, and taking risks (Jaskyte, 2004).

In my experience working with many nonprofits I found that the values of stability, teamwork, and people orientation are reflected in the sense of community prevalent in the typical nonprofit organization. I have found that people who are motivated to work in the nonprofit field feel that environments marked by care, compassion, and support of fellow employees are reflective of their own values and compatible with the social mission of the organization. Although the conclusion cannot be drawn from one study, combined with experience, I believe a question to explore is whether there is an inherent tension between those values that encourage creativity and innovation, and those values often related to nonprofit cultures and workplace organizations.

Motivational Influences. The vast majority of individuals I have worked with who have chosen careers in nonprofit organizations are motivated by a drive to achieve social good or justice through their work. They see themselves as engaged in a common pursuit they believe will benefit society, and they are passionate about their work. In fact, upon entering their field of work, nonprofit employees may be among the most intrinsically motivated, which has been acknowledged as encouraging creative behavior. (Amabile, 1996). This, as opposed to extrinsic motivation, which is, in most circumstances, is not conducive to creativity. In discussing intrinsic motivation values of nonprofit or public service employees, Jaskyte (2014) built on the findings of Perry and Wise (1990) and concluded that public sector employees are motivated by "a set of altruistic motives, such as wanting to shape policies, effect social change, and serve public interest" (p. 286). Why then, do we generally not hear the buzzwords of creativity and innovation connected with nonprofit organizations?

It is my contention that what might be limiting creativity in the nonprofit environment is nonprofit board and management goal-setting that creates a focus on short-term program impact, fundraising results, and donor retention. Many nonprofit organizations are guided by the principle that donors expect and deserve an economically efficient impact on society in exchange for their donation. Boards generally consider this factor in carrying out their fiduciary duties. This results in two forces that I believe are contrary to the creative process: (1) pressure to meet set fundraising goals, and (2) pressure to ensure that programmatic initiatives demonstrate a successful impact within a relatively short period of time. The first factor, although not equal to a direct financial reward for labor, in effect correlates to whether employees will retain their jobs, as the majority of nonprofits are dependent on donations for financial sustainability. The second factor leaves little or no room for the creative principle of trying many things in order to achieve success. Both of these influences may in fact operate as sources of extrinsic motivation.

I found Amabile's (1996) maze analogy of the creative process helpful in understanding how such forms of extrinsic motivation may discourage creativity and innovation in a nonprofit environment. Thinking of each creativity task as a maze, with one entrance but many different exits and pathways to those exits, facing an extrinsic motivator (such as an expected reward, evaluation, or a time limit), the individual in the maze will try to seek out the fastest, most known workable route to get out. But, in order to develop creative solutions, the alternative pathways in the maze must be explored, and the environmental factors around the pathways must be assessed and responded to. Only when working with intrinsic motivation will individuals be willing to take the risk and time to focus on other routes out of the maze—in other words, innovative solutions to problems (Amabile, 1996; Hennessey, 2003). For nonprofits to foster innovative solutions, leaders must establish organizational climates that encourage their employees to spend a longer time in the maze. This will necessitate educating donors and other stakeholders about the need for innovation, as well as an understanding of what is necessary to foster creativity, including a willingness to devote time and financial resources to pathways that may not be a sure thing.

Conclusion

An understanding of creativity and innovation in nonprofit organizations is integral to society. Nonprofits have made many inroads into solving complex social problems, yet intractable challenges, such as persistent poverty and environmental issues, need new approaches to move the needle at a faster pace. Nonprofit organizations are uniquely positioned to undertake this work. To best serve in this role, nonprofit organizations need to embrace creativity, explore ideas, take risks, and imagine the future. Championing that understanding is an important area for creativity experts to provide some focus.

Research into the process of creativity and innovation in the nonprofit environment is called for—there is sufficient empirical and anecdotal evidence to draw the conclusion that, while the cognitive processes of creativity may not differ, the influencing factors and mechanisms that contribute to the process do. Factors such as organizational structure, stakeholder acceptance, and employee and board motivation are some that I believe worthy of exploration in connection with their potential for influencing creativity and innovation. But I do not place the burden solely on creativity practitioners; nonprofit leaders, staff members, and board members need to be an integral part of the learning process, for it is only through combined understanding and influence that nonprofit environments will successfully foster creativity and innovation. And for those privileged to have a deep connection with both the world of creativity and nonprofit work, the onus is on us to make the connection between creativity and the social change that nonprofit organizations seek.

References

Allen, S. L., Smith, J. E., & Da Silva, N. (2013). Leadership style in relation to organizational change and organizational creativity: Perceptions from nonprofit organizational members. *Nonprofit Management & Leadership, 24*(1), 23-42.

Amabile, T. M. (1996). *Creativity in context.* Boulder, CO: Westview Press.

Brooks, A. C. (2008). *Social entrepreneurship: A modern approach to social value creation.* Upper Saddle River, NJ: Prentice Hall.

Camillus, J. C. (2008, May). *Strategy as a wicked problem*. Retrieved from https://hbr.org/2008/05/strategy-as-a-wicked-problem

Chait, R. P., Ryan, W. P., & Taylor, B. E. (2005). *Governance as leadership: Reframing the work of nonprofit boards*. Hoboken, NJ: BoardSource, Inc.

Coombes, S. M. T., Morris, M. H., Allen, J. A., & Webb, J. W. (2011). Behavioural orientations of non-profit boards as a factor in entrepreneurial performance: Does governance matter? *Journal of Management Studies, 48*(4), 829-856.

Grimm, R., Fox, C., Baines, S., & Albertson, K. (2013). Social innovation, an answer to contemporary societal challenges? Locating the concept in theory and practice. *Innovation: The European Journal of Social Science Research, 26*(4), 436-455.

Gunn, R., & Durkin, C. (Eds.). (2010). *Social entrepreneurship: A skills approach*. Bristol, UK: The Policy Press.

Hennessey, B. A. (2003). The social psychology of creativity. *Scandinavian Journal of Educational Research, 47*(3), 253-271.

Isaksen, S. G., & Akkermans, H. J. (2011). Creative climate: A leadership lever for innovation. *Journal of Creative Behavior, 45*(3), 161-187.

Jaskyte, K. (2004). Transformational leadership, organizational culture, and innovativeness in nonprofit organizations. *Nonprofit Management & Leadership, 15*(2), 153–168.

Jaskyte, K. (2012). Boards of directors and innovation in nonprofit organizations. *Nonprofit Management & Leadership, 22*(4), 439-459.

Jaskyte, K. (2014). Individual and work values of nonprofit, public, and business employees: How similar or different are they? *Human Service Organizations: Management, Leadership & Governance, 38*(3), 283-296.

Jiang, M., & Thagard, P. (2014). Creative cognition in social innovation. *Creativity Research Journal, 26*(4), 375-388.

Morris, M. H., Coombes, S. M. T., Allen, J., & Schindehutte, M. (2007). Antecedents and outcomes of entrepreneurial and market orientations in a non-profit context: Theoretical and empirical insights. *Journal of Leadership & Organizational Studies, 13*(4), 12-39.

Mumford, M. D. (2002). Social innovation: Ten cases from Benjamin Franklin. *Creativity Research Journal, 14*(2), 253-266.

Perry, J. L., & Wise, L. R. (1990). The motivational bases of public service. *Public Administration Review, 50*(3), 367-373.

Phills Jr., J. A., Deiglmeier, K., & Miller, D. T. (2008). Rediscovering social innovation. *Stanford Social Innovation Review, 6*(4), 33-43.

Puccio, G. J., Mance, M., & Murdock, M. C. (2011). *Creative leadership: Skills that drive change* (2nd ed.). Thousand Oaks, CA: SAGE Publications.

Rittel, H., & Webber, M. M. (1973). Dilemmas in a general theory of planning. *Policy Sciences, 4*, 155-169.

Say Yes to Education Buffalo. (n.d.). *Say Yes Buffalo.* Retrieved from http://sayyesbuffalo.org/

WNY Women's Foundation. (n.d.). *MOMs: From education to employment.* Retrieved from https://wnywomensfoundation.org/work/moms-from-education-to-employment/

About the Author

Jacobs is well-known in the Western New York community for her philanthropic leadership of numerous community organizations. She is a founding member and the chair emeritus of the WNY Women's Foundation. She also serves on the Elmwood Franklin School Board of Trustees and is a board member of the Community Foundation for Greater Buffalo, where she chairs the Governance Committee, co-chairs the Strategic Planning Committee, and serves on the Impact Committee. She is a past member and treasurer of the Buffalo Seminary Board of Trustees, a former board member and vice president of the Maria Love Convalescent Fund, and a past member of the boards of the Roswell Park Alliance Foundation and the Junior League of Buffalo. She and her husband, Jeremy Jacobs, Jr., co-chaired the United Way Annual Campaign.

Jacobs earned her Bachelor of Arts degree from Colgate University and her Juris Doctorate from the University of Pennsylvania. She practiced corporate and business-related immigration law at Hodgson Russ LLP. She also holds a Graduate Certificate in Creativity and Change Leadership from the International Center for Studies in Creativity at SUNY Buffalo State.

CREATIVITY
& EDUCATION

What is the Relationship Between Creativity and Learning?

Sara Smith
International Center for Studies in Creativity
SUNY Buffalo State

Abstract

Creativity is often undervalued in education. It is perceived as optional. In reality, creativity and learning are highly interconnected; they depend on and cultivate each other. Both creativity and learning are cognitive processes and share underlying mechanisms and principles. A case is made for regarding creativity as a vital and dynamic pair to learning. Their inextricable link is demonstrated through theories of each, aspects of cognition, and factors that foster both creative thinking and learning. Viewing creativity in the context of learning provides a stronger picture of both and demonstrates the need for both to be worked towards with diligence. Eight recommendations for educators are distilled and offered.

What is the Relationship Between Creativity and Learning?

It was third grade state testing day. I was teaching third grade for the first time, so I only partially knew what to expect. I had followed the curriculum and given the practice tests. Now, I just had to see what would come of it. I had to hope that my efforts to teach them the content would serve them in solving the problems on the test. My students did fine – not amazing, not terrible – but one set of questions still bothers me to this day. It involved pattern blocks, the small colorful shapes often used in classrooms to learn math skills. As I walked around the room and watched some struggle with the problem, I realized how much better the children would have been able to answer it if I had given them more time to just play with the pattern blocks in class. If they had been given time to just explore the ways the blocks fit together and experimented with all the possibilities the blocks held, this question would have been second nature for them. Instead the blocks had been used specifically in class, when the curriculum called for it, and I had failed my students by not recognizing the value of creativity.

Several years later, I became a student of creativity. Since then I have not only fallen in love with creativity as a discipline, I have learned the indivisible connection it has to learning. Unfortunately, from my teaching days, I know all too well the corner that creativity can get swept into. Despite all of the important ways they are connected, learning and creativity are in completely different realms of priority in most schools. Learning is viewed as the primary point of education, while creativity is nice if you can fit it in, which is probably after the work of learning is complete. Many teachers only have vague notions of what creativity really means and therefore rely on common misconceptions like equating it with art. I have learned that creativity facilitates our learning and raises us to new heights. For the love of learning and creativity, I had to investigate this inextricable link. Once teachers, like the one I was, see the merit of creativity and its connection to deep learning, we can no longer accept it being undervalued.

Interconnection

Creativity and learning are both vital aspects of the human experience. They are also highly interconnected. Creativity requires and stimulates learning, and learning is where creativity begins and where it strives to go. They are both routes for change and, ultimately, avenues to create meaning on individual, societal, and historical scales. The more creativity and learning are allowed to naturally interconnect, the more fully they can both be expressed.

Creativity is the generation of something novel and useful (Runco & Jaeger, 2012; Stein, 1953). It reveals itself through problem-solving, creating visions of what could be, and combining previously unconnected ideas (Davis, 2004). It can be demonstrated in any domain and at any moment. By definition, learning is a change in behavior or knowledge based on experience (Seel, 2012). This big question focuses on the relationship between learning and creativity and how we can better appreciate the role creativity plays in learning. We will look at how learning leads to creativity, how creativity fuels learning, and how other factors affect both creativity and learning. Based on these relationships, eight recommendations for educators are provided.

A Continuous Cycle

Learning Leads to Creativity

Creativity and learning begin in the same moment: the spark of a new thought or a new understanding. At this moment, the potential is born for both further learning and higher levels of creativity. Kaufman and Beghetto (2009) described this learning moment as mini-c or the most basic stage of creativity. As creativity develops, it can become more sophisticated and farther reaching; mini-c is entirely personal, but further developed creativity influences wider and wider circles. While learning begins as a creative act, it also provides the foundation for further creativity. Amabile's (2012) model of creativity has three personal components: domain skills, creativity skills, and task motivation. Domain skills are the knowledge and understanding related to a domain or field. She argued that to generate creative thinking within a domain, one must have knowledge of that area to build upon. As a person gains more knowledge and is more capable of using their understanding to think creatively, Kaufman and Beghetto (2009) said they can demonstrate little-c creativity, the kind of creativity that can come about in everyday activities. Further creative development in life can then become professional level (Pro-c) creativity. Eventually, a person's creativity can change history (Big-C) and extend the reach of human learning. Without learning, creativity can never be conceived, and without creativity, learning has nowhere to go.

Bloom's taxonomy is a learning model that organizes learning objectives by levels of sophistication. In this model, a basic understanding of a concept involves remembering facts, and the highest level of a learner's attainment, as of the most recent revision, is "creating" (Krathwohl, 2002). Once a person has a solid grasp of facts and how to apply them, they demonstrate higher-level thinking by using that understanding to engage their creativity and develop something new. Bloom's taxonomy is often conceptualized as a triangle with the basic skills of remembering and understanding facts at the bottom because they support the higher-level skills of evaluating and creating. It is important to note that in Bloom's model, the goal is to continue to move higher up the triangle with regards to one's learning, creating a strong foundation that enables a learner to reach the pinnacle and create something new from their understanding.

These connections are generally easy for a teacher to see. The more we know, the more able we are to use our knowledge in creative ways. However, creativity also powers learning, even at the most basic of levels, which holds strong implications for our classrooms.

Creativity Fuels Learning

Connections. Creativity and learning both occur through mechanisms within the brain. Creativity has been shown to come about from making connections (Koestler, 1964; Scott, Leritz, & Mumford, 2004). For example, combining the concepts of a phone and a computer led to the widely influential innovation of the smartphone. This concept of combining ideas is related to the transfer of learning. In *How People Learn,* Bransford, Brown, and Cocking (2000) stated, "a major goal of schooling is to prepare students for flexible adaptation to new problems and settings" (p. 235). When we learn something, we need to be able to apply that learning in other settings and situations. Actively engaging with what we learn, exploring possibilities, and making connections with new information provides more opportunities for learning transfer. Constructivist and other modern conceptions of learning place the learner as an active player in constructing their knowledge based upon experiences within the world and building upon prior knowledge (Nathan & Sawyer, 2015). The more a person has stored in long-term memory, and the more their understanding is rooted in cognitively active experiences, the better able they are to use that knowledge to build upon for further learning. More connections mean more possible avenues for recalling something later. For example, a young girl may connect the score of the football games she loves to watch with the seven times table she is trying to learn. Suddenly her attempt at remembering her multiples of seven becomes decidedly easier. When people are allowed time to find connections between what they are learning and what they know or what they want to create, they are using the creativity skill of "making connections" to further their learning. As reported by the Organisation for Economic Co-operation and Development (OECD) (2016), math learners who employ elaboration strategies in which they "make connections among mathematics tasks, link...learning to their own prior knowledge and real-life situations, and find different ways of solving a problem" (p. 49) are more likely to solve the most challenging mathematical problems than those who use memorization strategies. Lindsey Richland, a cognitive scientist, explained, "The underpinnings of the ability to do higher-order thinking really comes down to reasoning about relationships" (as quoted in Boser, 2017). Finding patterns and making connections is an act of creativity that engages the brain and solidifies learning.

Default Mode Network. Current research into brain networks has revealed the importance of the Default Mode Network (DMN) to imagination and creativity. The default mode network includes the parts of the brain that become active when a person is not focused on a task. It is the network that has taken over just before you realize your mind is wandering. Seligman has nicknamed the DMN the "imagination network" (Imagination Institute, 2016). The DMN is responsible for the inwardly focused thoughts we have like imagining one's future, putting things in emotional context, and thinking autobiographically (Gotlieb, Jahner, Immordino-Yang, & Kaufman, 2016). It is a creative skill to envision a future and make the connections necessary to see that vision through. Gotlieb et al. (in press) suggested that the work of the DMN may also support deep learning. They have argued that while activation of the DMN is undesirable when completing tasks that load working memory, allowing for time to reflect on learned content can support the making of meaningful connections. In this way, the DMN may enable one to recognize the personal relevance of what is learned and apply it to the desired future. "Constructive internal reflection allows students to process information in terms of emotion and self, which facilitates the transfer of knowledge from a lecture to life" (Gotlieb et al., in press, p. 12). If you have paused at all while reading this to consider how this connects to your work or your child's school experience, you have used this creative mind-wandering to make personal connections. "Imagination facilitates creative, critical dispositions toward new content and skills by helping students conjure new connections between ideas and invent new ways to represent and apply information" (Gotlieb et al., in press, p. 2). This is how content gets embedded into a person's experience to be used again and in more sophisticated ways.

Seeing differently. Creativity is often about looking at some stimulus or piece of information from a new perspective or through a different lens. Creativity manifested in this way is connected with how we learn. Levels-of-processing theory describes how more elaborate analyses of information can improve the likelihood of remembering it (Smith & Kosslyn, 2007). Considering information from many angles, or "looking at it another way," as Torrance and Safter (1999) said, can provide for this deeper processing that assists in learning new information. Similarly, it is understood that people's working memory is limited. We can only deal with around seven pieces of information at once, or even less (Cowan, 2001; Miller, 1956). For example, if you were asked to memorize the following string of characters, DFWA TLSF OORD LGAD EN, you would probably have trouble after the first 5-9 characters when it was time to recall. However, if you saw it differently, perhaps in slightly different groupings, you would be able to recall it all much easier by remembering, for example, the airport codes around the United States. When given the time to see things creatively, our learning and memory can be enhanced. We also tend to learn more effectively when presented with something creative or unique. Novelty has been shown to be more likely to capture a person's attention and can improve perception, increase motivation, and positively affect learning (Schomaker & Meeter, 2015).

Creative process. Creativity is an iterative process, repeatedly cycling back into itself. When thinking creatively, we come up with an idea, develop it, implement it, test it, develop it some more, add other ideas, test it again, etc. The iterative characteristic of creativity can also be meaningful for learning and memory. Each iteration is an opportunity to strengthen learning. Research into memory is showing that repeated use of information in long-term memory increases that information's "retrieval strength" (goCognitive, 2012). The more we use and work with the knowledge we have, the stronger it becomes, and the better we can recall it for later use. The repeated cycles within creativity can help increase the availability of information that can be used to make novel connections and solidify the learning of such information all at once.

Creativity is often viewed as being brought about in response to a problem that needs a solution (Osborn, 1953). In fact, many models of creativity are problem-solving models (Puccio, Mance, & Murdock, 2011; Scott, Leritz, & Mumford, 2004). New ideas come about when conventional means are no longer effective responses to a problem. An important aspect of learning effectively that is served well by problem-solving is called the "generation effect" (Brown, Roediger, & McDaniel, 2014). People are better able to learn information if they struggle with the content first and generate the answer on their own. Opportunities for problem-solving allow a person to generate a solution themselves, which is like creating a path for oneself in the snow. Making your own footprints will help you find your way better in the future than just being beamed to the destination. Engaging in problem-solving requires us to pull information from long-term memory, strengthens our understanding of the domain content we are working with, and encourages more creative solutions at the same time.

Deliberate creativity. Metacognition is a much-revered aspect of learning because it is about understanding how to learn. Many studies have shown that metacognitive skill positively influences learning, including the development of expertise (Ericsson, Krampe, & Tesch-Römer, 1993; Papaleontiou-Louca, 2014). When we practice reflecting on our thinking and choosing effective strategies, our ability to learn new information increases. One way to exercise metacognition is through engaging in creative processes. Deliberate creative processes like Creative Problem Solving (Puccio, Mance, & Murdock, 2011) depend on this metacognitive ability, requiring a person to choose thinking strategies to employ and monitor their movement through the process. The set of creativity skills introduced by researchers Torrance and Safter (1999) is another example of metacognition in creativity. Being able to "break through boundaries" (Torrance & Safter, 1999) requires one to consider the constraints of one's own thinking and then deliberately look outside of them. Creative processes engage metacognition, which drives learning.

Factors That Affect Creativity and Learning

Creativity and learning are also interconnected in that the same underlying principles and mechanisms that feed creativity also feed learning. Creativity is often considered a mindset or attitude. Ruth Noller developed the creativity formula $C=fa(K,I,E)$, which demonstrated the idea that creativity is the function of one's attitude toward knowledge, imagination, and evaluation (Isaksen, Dorval, & Treffinger, 1994). In *Creativity is Forever*, Davis (2004) called creativity "a way of living and perceiving" the world (p. 2). If we make the effort to feed a creative attitude, learning will also be nourished. We can feed this attitude through play, motivation, and the way we think about ourselves and our experience.

Play. Play is characterized by positive affect, intrinsic motivation, and openness to possibility (Brown & Vaughan, 2009). It is considered a fundamental aspect of creativity, listed as an affective skill in the Thinking Skills Model of Creative Problem Solving (Puccio, Mance, & Murdock, 2011). Play is open-ended; it is the practice of seeing the world "as-if" and responding accordingly. It is taking the perspective of an imaginary character; it is being open to possibilities instead of locked into a specific outcome. The visioning (seeing things as they could be) and divergent thinking (generating many ideas) aspects of creativity are readily apparent when looking at play.

Gopnik and Walker (2013) called play "a type of exploratory learning" (p. 15). Play is present as an activity in every human culture and every normally developing child. It is highly motivating and provides a way to practice many skills. Starting with animal studies in the 1960s, research has shown that play assists in brain development. It promotes new connections between neurons, and it allows us to practice planning, interacting with others socially, regulating our emotions, and making judgments (Brown & Vaughan, 2009). In a study by Bonawitz, Shafto, Gweon, Goodman, Spelke, & Schulz (2011) children who were given the opportunity to freely explore an object were better able to find new uses and functions for a toy than those that were instructed in just one function, demonstrating that play can open possibilities for learning and discovery. Sawyer (2004) has advocated the significance of people learning through emergent processes, meaning those in which the specific outcome is unpredictable, a characteristic of creativity and play.

Mindset. Dweck (2006) has researched mindset and its effect on people's lives. She has found two different ways people think about their creative abilities and intelligence. A fixed mindset is one that views one's abilities as inborn and static; a growth mindset sees creativity and intelligence as qualities that can be enhanced and worked towards (Dweck, 2006). Instead of seeing failures or challenges as examples of a lack of ability, a person with a growth mindset sees them as opportunities for learning and developing more skill. This person is resilient in the face of unexpected obstacles. Someone with a growth mindset, Dweck (2006) explained, is also more likely to engage in the deliberate practice that is important for learning and developing expertise and more willing to employ creativity.

Creativity and learning both require a state of mind that is open and vulnerable; for each process, we must be willing to dive into the unknown. Creativity requires risk-taking and tolerance of ambiguity as new territory is charted (Puccio, Mance, & Murdock, 2011). This tolerance for ambiguity can also help in learning, as evidence suggests believing knowledge is uncertain and can be ambiguous leads to more effective learning (Schommer, 1990). An active learner must also be vulnerable by admitting that they do not know something before they can learn something new. Putting oneself in the place of receiving feedback is an act of vulnerability that is an important part of both processes. Feedback guides a person through the iterative process of creativity. It allows creative ideas to be improved upon and further developed and allows the creator to be even more creative. In reference to learning, Hattie (2008) called feedback "the most powerful single influence enhancing achievement" (p. 12). Fear of failure or resistance to vulnerability and ambiguity can cause learning to stall. It can also block creativity and end the learning-creativity cycle.

Motivation. Intrinsic motivation is a central component to both creativity and learning. Intrinsic motivation is the desire to engage in an activity for the sake of the activity itself and an internal feeling of satisfaction (Hon, 2012). Intrinsic motivation has consistently been demonstrated to relate to creativity in research studies (Amabile, 1996). One of the foremost researchers on intrinsic motivation, Amabile (2012), has found it to be so vital to creativity that it is one of the components in her componential model of creativity. Without motivation to complete a task, the higher levels of thought associated with creativity are unlikely to occur. Learning is also driven by intrinsic motivation. Decades of research indicate that intrinsic motivation is an important factor in learning effectiveness and is preferable to extrinsic motivation for the development of self-regulation, an aspect of learning (Deci & Ryan, 2009; Deci, Ryan, &

Koestner, 1999). Being aware of motivation and fostering intrinsic motivation in learning environments sets the foundation for creativity and learning to occur.

Where Do We Go From Here?

Educators know they need to support deep learning in their students as well as encourage them to use mastered knowledge in new ways. Fortunately, these goals are not as disparate as schools have often treated them, and the way to reach both is through valuing and harnessing creativity. For too long creativity has been pushed to the side to work on the learning part first, but when we effectively articulate the degree of connection between learning and creativity, it becomes clear that learning environments must hold the two as equals. It is both short-sighted and less productive to strive for learning without also striving for creativity. They need each other to create that upward spiral of growth, in an individual and in the world. There is a long road ahead yet in education to get to the point where creativity is maximized in our students, but based on the creativity-learning connection we've outlined, here are some steps educators can take in their classrooms to get started.

1. Encourage the making of connections between ideas, subjects, and situations. Connections are the lifeblood of creativity and learning.

2. Give time for reflection and even a little daydreaming. Allowing students to see content in personally meaningful ways helps them remember it and use it more effectively and creatively.

3. Encourage seeing things from a new perspective and trying something a different way. Don't get bogged down in the "correct" way or answer. Even if a new idea doesn't work, it provides another avenue for remembering and using the content.

4. Engage in longer-term problem-solving processes. Time to work through an issue or challenge gives opportunities to continually use content knowledge toward a goal, making learning more effective.

5. Deliberately employ creativity strategies and processes in class. It develops metacognitive skills that are the basis for successful learning and brings creativity to the forefront of how the classroom runs.

6. Value and utilize students' personal interests and motivation. They are more likely to both learn and be creative when they gain internal satisfaction from it.

7. Allow time for play. This gives opportunities to make connections, see things differently, and draw on motivation in addition to the myriad social and emotional benefits.

8. Teach them how their brain works and that effort means their brains are growing. Give them specific, useful feedback and model the spirit of being vulnerable in the name of improvement.

The Ultimate Goal

As we have seen, learning engages creativity at its start and holds creativity as its highest expression. The reason creativity is the goal of learning is because it causes us to re-enter the cycle of learning. Take, for example, Albert Einstein, whose theory of relativity was not the end of human learning about the universe but the beginning of a whole new level of possibility for human learning. Creativity starts with learning, requires learning, and is powered by learning. In turn, creativity drives further learning.

The ultimate goal of both creativity and learning is growth. Both instigate change within our brains and have the capacity to create change on a wider scale because they feed each other and cause an upward spiral of increasing learning and creativity. Both allow us to make meaning out of everything around us. Individually, we learn to find our unique contribution to the world based on our strengths, experiences, and motivations. The more we learn and create, the more impactful our contributions can be.

References

Amabile, T. M. (1996). *Creativity in context*. Boulder, CO: Westview Press.

Amabile, T. M. (2012). *Componential theory of creativity* (Working Paper No. 12-096). Boston, MA: Harvard Business School. https://doi.org/http://dx.doi.org/10.4135/9781452276090.n42

Bonawitz, E., Shafto, P., Gweon, H., Goodman, N. D., Spelke, E., & Schulz, L. (2011). The double-edged sword of pedagogy: Instruction limits spontaneous exploration and discovery. *Cognition*, *120*(3), 322–330. https://doi.org/10.1016/j.cognition.2010.10.001

Bransford, J. D., Brown, A. L., & Cocking, R. R. (Eds.). (2000). *How people learn: Brain, mind, experience, and school*. Washington, DC: National Academy of Sciences.

Brown, P. C., Roediger, H. L., & McDaniel, M. A. (2014). *Make it stick: The science of successful learning.* Cambridge, MA: The Belknap Press of Harvard University Press.

Brown, S. L., & Vaughan, C. C. (2009). *Play: How it shapes the brain, opens the imagination, and invigorates the soul.* New York, NY: Avery.

Cowan, N. (2001). The magical number 4 in short-term memory: A reconsideration of mental storage capacity. *Behavioral and Brain Sciences.* 24: 1–185.

Davis, G. A. (2004). *Creativity is forever.* Dubuque, IA: Kendall/Hunt.

Deci, E. L., & Ryan, R. (2009). Intrinsic motivation: Definition and directions. *Academy of Management Learning and Education, 8*(2), 225–237. https://doi.org/10.1006/ceps.1999.1020

Deci, E. L., Ryan, R. M., & Koestner, R. (1999). A meta-analytic review of experiments examining the effects of extrinsic rewards on intrinsic motivation. *Psychological Bulletin, 125*(6), 627–668. https://doi.org/10.1037/0033-2909.125.6.627

Dweck, C. S. (2006). *Mindset: The new psychology of success.* New York, NY: Random House.

Ericsson, K. A., Krampe, R. T., & Tesch-Römer, C. (1993). The role of deliberate practice in the acquisition of expert performance. *Psychological Review, 100*(3), 363-406.

goCognitive. (2012, June 12). *Robert Bjork: Storage strength vs. retrieval strength.* [Video file]. Retrieved from: http://www.gocognitive.net/interviews/storage-strength-vs-retrieval-strength

Gopnik, A., & Walker, C. M. (2013). Considering counterfactuals: The relationship between causal learning and pretend play. *American Journal of Play, 6*(1), 15–28.

Gotlieb, R., Jahner, E., Immordino-Yang, M. H., & Kaufman, S. B. (2016). How social-emotional imagination facilitates deep learning and creativity in the classroom. In R. A. Beghetto & J. C. Kaufman (Eds.). *Nurturing creativity in the classroom* (2nd Ed.). New York, NY: Cambridge University Press.

Hattie, J. (2008). *Visible learning: A synthesis of over 800 meta-analyses relating to achievement.* New York, NY: Routledge.

Hon, A. H. Y. (2012). Shaping environments conductive to creativity: The role of intrinsic motivation. *Cornell Hospitality Quarterly, 53*(1), 53-64. doi:10.1177/1938965511424725

Imagination Institute. (2016, March). *Education imagination retreat*. [Video file]. Retrieved from: https://blogs.scientificamerican.com/beautiful-minds/how-can-education-foster-imagination-and-creativity/

Isaksen, S. G., Dorval, K. B., & Treffinger, D. J. (1994). *Creative approaches to problem solving*. Dubuque, IA: Kendall/Hunt.

Kaufman, J. C., & Beghetto, R. A. (2009). Beyond big and little: The four c model of creativity. *Review of General Psychology, 13*(1), 1–12. https://doi.org/10.1037/a0013688

Koestler, A. (1964). *The act of creation*. New York, NY: Dell.

Krathwohl, D. R. (2002). A revision of Bloom's taxonomy: An overview. *Theory into Practice, 41*(4), 212-218. doi:10.1207/s15430421tip4104_2

Miller, G. A. (1956). The magical number seven, plus or minus two: Some limits on our capacity for processing information. *Psychological Review, 63*(2), 81-97. http://dx.doi.org/10.1037/h0043158

Nathan, M. J., & Sawyer, R. K. (2015). Foundations of the learning sciences. In R. K. Sawyer (Ed.), *The Cambridge handbook of the learning sciences*. (2nd ed., pp. 21-33). New York, NY: Cambridge University Press.

OECD. (2016). *Ten questions for mathematics teachers and how PISA can help answer them*. Paris, France: OECD Publishing. http://dx.doi.or/10.1787/9789264265387-en

Osborn, A. F. (1957). *Applied imagination: Principles and procedures of creative thinking*. New York, NY: Charles Scribner's Sons.

Papaleontiou-Louca, E. (2014). Metacognition. In D. Phillips (Ed.), *Encyclopedia of educational theory and philosophy* (Vol. 2, pp. 523-525). Thousand Oaks, CA: SAGE Publications. doi: 10.4135/9781483346229.n218

Puccio, G., Mance, M., & Murdock, M. C. (2011). *Creative leadership: Skills that drive change*. (2nd ed.). Thousand Oaks, CA: SAGE Publications.

Runco, M. A., & Jaeger, G. J. (2012). The standard definition of creativity. *Creativity Research Journal, 24*(1), 92–96. https://doi.org/10.1080/10400419.2012.650092

Sawyer, R. K. (2004). Creative teaching: Collaborative discussion as disciplined improvisation. *Educational Researcher, 33*(2), 12-20.

Schomaker, J., & Meeter, M. (2015). Short- and long-lasting consequences of novelty, deviance and surprise on brain and cognition. *Neuroscience and Biobehavioral Reviews, 55*, 268-279. doi:10.1016/j.neubiorev.2015.05.002

Schommer, M. (1990). Effects of beliefs about the nature of knowledge on comprehension. *Journal of Educational Psychology, 82*(3), 498-504. doi:10.1037/0022-0663.82.3.498

Scott, G., Leritz, L. E., & Mumford, M. D. (2004). The effectiveness of creativity training: A quantitative review. *Creativity Research Journal, 16*(4), 361-388. doi:10.1080/10400410409534549

Seel, N. M. (2012). *Encyclopedia of the sciences of learning.* Boston, MA: Springer US. doi:10.1007/978-1-4419-1428-6

Smith, E. E., & Kosslyn, S. M. (2007). *Cognitive psychology: Mind and brain.* Upper Saddle River, NJ: Pearson/Prentice Hall.

Stein, M. I. (1953). Creativity and culture. *Journal of Psychology, 36*, 31–322.

Torrance, E. P., & Safter, H. T. (1999). *Making the creative leap beyond.* Buffalo, NY: Creative Education Foundation Press.

About the Author

Sara Smith has a Master of Science in creativity from the International Center for Studies in Creativity. She is a writer, creativity educator, and former elementary school teacher. Her experience in the classroom led her to the field of creativity and fueled her interest to support schools in cultivating creativity in teachers and students. Sara also leads local and online communities that focus on creativity and learning.

Find some of her work at www.creativityathome.com

Is Self-Directed Education the Answer to the Creativity Crisis?

Nicole Colter
International Center for Studies in Creativity
SUNY Buffalo State

Abstract

This paper examines the creativity crisis and its effects on our children and our future. It explains Self-Directed Education (SDE) and reviews its history. It looks at the role of intrinsic motivation in creativity and learning and proposes an *Intrinsic Motivation Principle of Learning.* The interrelationships of educative drives and self-determination needs are explored. The author asserts that SDE is the answer to the creativity crisis.

Is Self-Directed Education the Answer to the Creativity Crisis?

My youngest daughter's academic struggle started in first grade. By middle school, she was defeated, depressed, and starting to change in a way that was heart-breaking. She shredded her self-esteem by comparing herself to others; we were losing her bit by bit. After two unsuccessful years at two different high schools, I considered a form of Self-Directed Education (SDE) called unschooling, in which children don't go to school and instead are given freedom to explore the world in whatever way they choose (Farenga, 2016). I had recently heard of the concept and loved the idea, but I didn't trust her, myself, or our relationship to bear the full responsibility for her education; I regret that. The last two years were better, but too little too late. She launched into the world unprepared to "adult." Her strengths, which are mostly creative, were never acknowledged or developed in school, and her weaknesses, despite the school's aggressive attempts, were never remediated. I wish this was an isolated story, but it isn't: I worked in a high school for three years and saw this pattern repeated over and over again. We can do better. Our children, and our world, deserve better.

E. Paul Torrance, considered the father of creativity in education, articulated the words that would become the *Manifesto for Children* after reflecting on the findings of his 22-year longitudinal study of creative behavior of children into adulthood. The manifesto reads:

> Don't be afraid to fall in love with something and pursue it with intensity. Know, understand, take pride in, practice, develop, exploit, and enjoy your greatest strengths. Learn to free yourself from the expectations of others and to walk away from the games they impose on you. Free yourself to play your own game. Find a great teacher or mentor who will help you. Don't waste energy trying to be well-rounded. Do what you love and can do well. Learn the skills of interdependence. (Torrance, 1983b)

Imagine if every child was read this at bedtime or the start of each school day. Imagine how much more creative children might become if more parents and teachers supported and empowered children to live this way. Sadly, this is not happening. Instead, America is facing a creativity crisis (Kim, 2011).

But what if the creativity crisis could be averted through SDE? This paper will examine the creativity crisis and explain SDE. It will unpack intrinsic motivation in relation to creativity and learning and explain how SDE can end this crisis.

The Creativity Crisis

Creative thinking in Americans of all ages has continually declined since 1990; the biggest drops are in children in grades K-3, with the second largest drop in children in grades 4-6 (Kim, 2011). After a thorough analysis of decades of Torrance Test of Creative Thinking (TTCT; Torrance, 1966) scores, Kim (2011) concluded that beginning around 1990, younger children were tending to grow up

> less emotionally expressive, less energetic, less talkative and verbally expressive, less humorous, less imaginative, less unconventional, less lively and passionate, less perceptive, less apt to connect seemingly irrelevant things, less synthesizing, and less likely to see things from a different angle…steadily losing their ability to elaborate upon ideas… less capable of the critical thinking processes of synthesis and organization and less capable of capturing the essence of problems [and] more narrow-minded, less intellectually curious, and less open to new experiences. (p. 292)

Kim (2017) found that the creativity crisis has gotten even worse since 2008. Creative abilities are not being nurtured in childhood, ultimately creating a society of stunted adults (Kim, 2011). Can SDE nurture these creative abilities and end this crisis?

What is Self-Directed Education?

Life is our greatest creative teacher; lessons are abundant everywhere, every day. When we are first born we start to learn by doing. We make connections in context and learn through repeated failure before success. Parents and facilitators of SDE seek to provide the environment that keeps learning a natural part of life past early childhood.

The Alliance for Self-Directed Education (ASDE, n.d.-a) offers the definition driving this paper: "Self-Directed Education is education that derives from the *self-chosen* activities and life experiences of the person becoming educated, *whether or not those activities were chosen deliberately for the purpose of education* [emphasis added]" (para. 5).

The SDE philosophy can be traced back to A.S. Neill, who founded the Summerhill Boarding School in England in 1921, and Daniel Greenberg, who founded Sudbury Valley School in Massachusetts in 1968 (Gray, 2017). This philosophy gained traction in the 1970s when John Holt coined the term *unschooling* (Farenga, 2016). There are also a small number of public schools, usually alternative, democratic, or free schools, where SDE is taking place (Gray, 2017), but it has predominantly taken place through the unschooling form of homeschooling. Today, the homeschooling movement is growing rapidly (Farenga, 2016) and SDE is poised to grow as well, due in part to the founding of the Alliance for Self-Directed Education in 2016, and the growth of SDE centers, micro-schools, and unschooling cooperatives. While there are many differences between SDE environments and the standard school model, one of the most prominent is the underlying motivation for learning (Riley, 2015).

The Role of Motivation in Learning

There is no question that students who perform well in school are usually motivated. Good grades are often a motivator for these students. Since grades are comparative, they may be motivated to do better than their classmates, or at least to not get a bad grade. They may be motivated to avoid failure. They may want to make their teachers and parents happy; maybe they will even get a special treat if they do well. These are extrinsic rewards based on external evidence of performance, and there is a limit to the benefits of this type of motivation (Amabile, 1998; Grolnick & Ryan, 1987; Ryan & Deci, 2017).

The limit of extrinsic motivation is evident in underperforming students. Who hasn't heard the dismissive complaint that "kids just aren't motivated anymore"? The real question to consider is "What *else* is motivating these students?" Kim (2011) attributed underachievement to schools' inabilities to meet students' creative needs. Kim and Hull (2012) found a strong correlation between higher levels of creativity and the odds of dropout. I believe that many underperforming students are simply not motivated toward the goals established by school but can feel strong intrinsic motivation towards personally meaningful goals which would meet their own creative needs. Therefore, focusing on intrinsic motivation is a better option for all students.

Intrinsic Motivation Principle of Learning

> *"Learning, by its very nature, is a creative act"*
> – Sandy Speicher (2017, para. 17)

The importance of intrinsic motivation to creativity has been documented for decades (Amabile, 1983, 1998; Hennessey, 2010; Ryan & Deci, 2017), as is the relationship between intrinsic motivation and learning (Grolnick & Ryan, 1987; Ryan & Deci, 2000, 2017). Amabile (1998) even articulated an Intrinsic Motivation Principle of Creativity: "people will be most creative when they feel motivated primarily by the interest, satisfaction, and challenge of the work itself—and not by external pressures" (p. 79). This paper extends Amabile's principle to the creative act of learning and proposes an *Intrinsic Motivation Principle of Learning*: people will *learn* the most when they feel motivated by the interest, satisfaction, and challenge of the exploration itself—and not by external pressures.

Unfortunately, many classrooms are not designed to optimize intrinsic motivation, which can diminish both learning and creativity. Hennessey (2015) espoused the influence of the classroom environment in supporting or undermining student motivation. Her frustration at the current state of affairs is evident. She stated, "expected rewards, expected evaluation, competition, time limits, and surveillance—how is it that this laundry list of killers of student intrinsic motivation and creativity reads like the recipe for the typical contemporary American classroom?" (Hennessey, 2015, p. 188). Her conclusion is supportive of SDE, encouraging training so that educators could learn "how best to serve as a facilitator of students' self-directed and active learning" (Hennessey, 2015, p. 191).

Self-Determination Theory (SDT), developed by Deci and Ryan (1985), considers intrinsic motivation to be inborn, the "human tendency toward learning and creativity" (Ryan & Deci, 2000, p. 69). Cognitive Evaluation Theory (CET), a sub-theory of SDT, specifies autonomy, competence, and relatedness as three essential nutrients in an intrinsically motivating environment (Ryan & Deci, 2000). Autonomy is "the need to self-regulate one's experiences and actions" (Ryan & Deci, 2017, p. 10). When people do something because they feel they have to, rather than choose to, it is called *external perceived locus of causality* and they feel controlled or manipulated like a pawn; true autonomy in relation to intrinsic motivation is *internal perceived locus of causality*—it is when you voluntarily, willfully engage and self-endorse an activity (de Charms, 1968). Competence refers to feeling capable and having a sense of mastery around the things in your life (Ryan & Deci, 2017); it has a lot in common with self-efficacy (Bandura, 1989). Relatedness refers to feeling cared for and socially connected;

it is belonging and feeling that you truly matter (Ryan & Deci, 2017). These are three needs of the psyche, and the greater an environment meets these needs, the more intrinsically motivated the individual will be (Ryan & Deci, 2000).

How Self-Directed Education Can Solve the Creativity Crisis

The success of SDE is not built on a specific formulaic curriculum; it is built on harnessing the natural learning process of children, a process driven by intrinsic motivation. Young children learn very challenging things in their first few years simply because they are curious, playful, and sociable (ASDE, n.d.-b, para. 1). These three educative drives produce monumental feats, such as walking and talking, without instruction.

Intrinsic motivation can be optimized by supporting these three educative drives in an environment that meets autonomy, competence, and relatedness needs. While all learning environments may proclaim to support these drives and needs, there is clearly a greater level of autonomy extended to children in SDE than in the standard school model. It is this difference that really sets SDE apart and provides the means to support all of the other drives and needs of children, and ultimately adults, to the fullest extent. Let's explore the relationships between these drives and needs, and their effects on intrinsic motivation (and therefore creativity and learning), in greater detail.

Curiosity and Playfulness

Human beings seem to be born rather curious. Play starts between mother and baby, establishes the basis for human trust, and is important for brain development and learning (S. Brown, 2008). Children are innately powered by curiosity; if given the freedom to explore and play, the result is "self regulation, curiosity, increased perseverance, progressive mastery and optimism" (Brown, 2014, para. 4). Play allows children to explore and test possibilities, learn to build things, role-play, collaborate, and make and follow rules (T. Brown, 2008).

SDE proposes that the self-chosen activities of children should be the starting point for learning. A counterargument may be that children, if left to choose, would play video games all day. Craft (2011) focused on the changing nature of childhood in the digital age and explained how children are being empowered by the pluralities, possibilities, participation, and playfulness of online and virtual spaces. She stated:

> The digital environment is a space which offers many possibilities for learning by doing and doing by learning. In other words, it is a space where projects and ideas can be generated and developed and where mistakes can be made and learned from. (Craft, 2011, p. 63)

Despite valid concerns about the impact of video game usage, there are actually extensive benefits (Craft, 2011; Gray, 2013), including how multiplayer online role-playing games allow children to flex their creativity and problem-solving muscles in impressive ways (Gray, 2013). Even though activities are ideally chosen by the child in SDE, in the case of video games, many parents and facilitators may negotiate some boundaries and provide explanations so the child can autonomously endorse those boundaries.

Gray (2013) argued that curiosity provides the motivation for learning, while playfulness provides the motivation to practice towards mastery. Curiosity is important to creativity, so an environment that allows a child to follow their curiosity will also help that child naturally develop their creativity (Phillips, 2014). Ekvall (1996) found playfulness to be important even in creative work environments for adults. How much more important might it be to keeping creativity alive for children? The National Institute for Play believes that if we apply the science of play we can transform education (National Institute for Play, n.d.), and that's exactly what SDE does.

Competence

When a child's curiosity drives their education, they are much more likely to follow their own interests, discover their own strengths, and work to their optimal level of challenge. This is part of the search for identity which Torrance (2002) considered "one of the most important things that a person ever does" (p. 32). Torrance (1983a) found that adults with the most creative achievements had fallen in love with something at an early age and pursued that.

However, Waters (2017) warned that "we may feel so pressured to help our children grow into the person society says they *should* be that we may not be allowing them to grow into the person they actually *are*" (p. 5). Waters (2017) explained how strengths develop over time; early childhood play and exploration allow children to have fun with potential strengths. Signs of strengths in a specific area are frequency of use, above-average functioning, and engagement in the activity or skill (Waters, 2017). By supporting our children's strengths, we can help them meet their competence need and build confidence, greater levels of happiness, better performance, increased self-esteem, enhanced ability to handle adversity, and reduced risk of depression (Waters, 2017). Supporting strengths helps children's self-efficacy and allows them to develop the tools to take control of their own lives (Waters, 2017). This approach also helps children develop optimism and resilience (Waters, 2017); sadly, schools tend to take the opposite approach, attempting instead to eliminate weaknesses.

Gallup (2014), through their student engagement poll, found that students whose schools and teachers built strengths and got them excited about the future were almost 30 times more likely to be engaged in their learning than students whose schools and teachers did not. Unfortunately, less than half of students reported getting to do what they do best every day at school (Gallup, 2014), which negatively affects motivation and enthusiasm about learning. Gallup (2014) recommended that schools employ a strengths-based approach and personalize students' education plans.

SDE allows children to immerse themselves in their strengths and stay engaged long enough to fall in love with something and provides the time necessary to develop those strengths and passions to the fullest extent. SDE is the solution that allows each child to individualize their learning so they can do their creative best with their own life.

Sociability and Relatedness

Children learn through social interaction, and so a valid concern frequently raised about SDE is that children will be socially isolated. However, Riley (2015) found no difference in relatedness satisfaction between young adults who had been educated in the standard school model and those that were homeschooled. The rise in SDE centers, micro-schools, and unschool cooperatives are creating SDE learning communities, which will expand and enrich the relationships of unschooled children.

In my experience with both SDE and Creative Problem Solving (CPS; Osborn, 1953), I have observed that the facilitators of both processes have much in common: they stay out of the content, help the child or client get unstuck, and are most successful when they can embody playfulness. Torrance (1979) captured the essence of the facilitator's relationship in SDE when he said:

> In this creative relationship a parent, teacher, counselor, or therapist must be willing to permit one thing to lead to another, to be ready to get off the beaten track or to break out of the mold, and to *relate to the child as a person* [emphasis added]. (p. 75)

Torrance (1979) went on to explain that it is "only when the child is convinced that you are not trying to reform him that he is able to open up and behave creatively" (p. 79). Yet this open, trusting relationship goes beyond creative behavior: it is important for the development of the whole child. Since SDE is strengths-based and assessment is not comparative, the relationship between child and parent or facilitator is much more relational and nurturing than is possible in the standard school model. This is vitally important for an intrinsically motivating environment.

There is no evidence that suggests that command-and-control, coercive education is good for children or learning. While skeptics of SDE on social media seem to believe that it will breed self-indulged children who have no respect; the reality is quite the contrary. Aaron Eden, education innovator and designer of LEAP Academy, an open-source school-within-a-school model built on the principles of SDE, believes the term *co-creative learning* better describes the relationship in SDE. According to Eden, "Self-Directed Education doesn't work *outside* of a healthy connected environment...it doesn't work through neglect and permissiveness. It works through a strong community that has within it the means to negotiate shared, parallel and divergent goals" (A. Eden, personal communication, November 22, 2017). All children deserve to pursue their interests freely in collaboration with and alongside others in a caring environment where they truly matter; this is *the pursuit of happiness* our democracy guarantees all people.

Autonomy and Planfulness

Children are born with the three educative drives of curiosity, playfulness, and sociability but the fourth educative drive, planfulness, develops over time (ASDE, n.d.-b). Once a child has a vision of their future, whether that future is tomorrow, next week, next year, or even longer, that child is inherently interested in planning for that future. She will take the steps necessary to make her desired future happen (ASDE, n.d.-b). Assuming she has not lacked autonomy throughout childhood, she is unlikely to see this responsibility as anyone else's but her own.

The rise in parental fear over the last decades means children are under almost constant surveillance (Gray, 2013) and are rarely in charge of their own lives. Barker et al. (2014) found the more unstructured time a child experienced, the greater that child's self-directed executive functioning. Most school interventions seek to improve children's externally-driven executive function, "where they are instructed on what goal-directed actions to carry out and when," as opposed to self-directed executive function, "where they must determine on their own what goal-directed actions to carry out and when" (Barker et al., 2014, p. 1). The latter seems more sophisticated, and more needed today, than the former. Self-directed executive function is connected to the CPS process executive step, *Assessing the Situation*, which requires being able to decide where to begin and when to make changes (Puccio, Mance, & Murdock, 2011). Therefore, self-directed executive function is important for both learning and creativity.

Many people are concerned that giving full autonomy to children means they won't learn the basics. Gray (2013) pointed out that children often attempt to emulate what they see; activities that are truly important, like reading and math, are such an integral part of life that unschoolers and children in SDE centers learn them rapidly, when they are ready. It would not be surprising, for example, for an unschooler to learn fractions while baking.

Autonomy is important to creativity (Amabile, 1998; Ekvall, 1996; Ryan & Deci, 2017) and learning (Grolnick & Ryan, 1987; Ryan & Deci, 2017). It allows a child to follow his curiosity and choose play, video games, or whatever other means of learning that sparks his interests. These "integrated and self-endorsed" actions provide greater "access to the person's cognitive, affective, and physical capacities" which impacts performance, behavior, and creativity (Ryan & Deci, 2017, p. 97). In this way, each child is able to grow into the unique, integrated, and whole (Ryan, 1993) individual that many adults spend their entire lives trying to find or recover.

Recommendations for Further Research

Schools were designed before we knew much about how people learn, and educational research predominantly focuses on how to better deliver the current school model (Sawyer, 2008). A relatively new field of interdisciplinary study called the learning sciences looks at teaching and learning in formal and informal settings and includes "cognitive science, educational psychology, computer science, anthropology, sociology, information sciences, neurosciences, education, design studies, instructional design, and other fields" (Sawyer, 2008, p. 45). Sawyer (2008) recommended that existing schools work closely with self-directed, informal, and non-school learning environments to redesign for the future. Education systems and the learning sciences researchers alike would benefit from looking at new SDE models such as Agile Learning Centers, LEAP Academy, Liberated Learners Network, and the student-designed, student-run, school-within-a-school called the Independent Project, which reads like a page from the learning sciences handbook itself (Levin & Engel, 2016).

For the link between SDE and creativity, we need data on how self-directed students score on measures of creativity, motivation, problem solving, and creative self-efficacy. We should compare SDE environments against creative environment measures such as Ekvall's 10 climate dimensions for creativity (1996) and Amabile's KEYS (1995). It would behoove us to develop a creative environment scale specifically for educational environments. I suspect many SDE principles would be represented in such a measure. Further research can be done into the role of autonomy in creativity and learning, and much could be gleaned from studying the facilitator-student dynamic within SDE and how it may encourage creative development.

Conclusion

Like many young adults, my daughter is going to have to find her way without a strong education foundation built on her creative strengths. We will continue to work together to develop the creativity skills I wish she had had the chance to cultivate in her school years. How many more children will endure a similar struggle? Are we ready to do better for the next generation?

The creativity crisis is one of many crises that will not get any better if we fail to protect and nurture creativity through disruptive changes in education. We have no idea what the future holds, but we know it will require creativity. Making children passive consumers of content for twelve or more years not only makes learning less effective, it also fails to cultivate the creative skillsets that children need to navigate the changes of the future.

SDE may seem like an extreme change, but this is how active learning took place for most of history. It extends the natural learning process of childhood and develops the self-directed executive function needed in adulthood. It is Torrance's (1983b) *Manifesto for Children* brought to life. The SDE environment supports curiosity, playfulness, responsible autonomy, strengths development, and healthy relationships, among many other benefits to learning, creativity, and well-being. Education customized by the students themselves is optimized for intrinsic motivation and promotes lifelong self-directed learning. If we want motivated, creative, lifelong learners, then mainstream education should seek to adopt SDE principles, as SDE is the creative education answer we've been looking for!

References

Amabile, T. M. (1983). The social psychology of creativity: A componential conceptualization. *Journal of Personality and Social Psychology, 45(2),* 357-376.

Amabile, T. M. 1995. KEYS: Assessing the climate for creativity. Instrument published by the Center for Creative Leadership, Greensboro, NC.

Amabile, T. M. (1998). How to kill creativity. *Harvard Business Review, 76(5),* 76-87.

Alliance for Self-Directed Education. (n.d.-a). *What is Self-Directed Education?* Retrieved from https://www.self-directed.org/sde

Alliance for Self-Directed Education. (n.d.-b). *The four educative drives.* Retrieved from https://www.self-directed.org/sde/drives/

Bandura, A. (1989). Human agency in social cognitive theory. *American Psychologist, 44*(9), 1175–1184.

Barker, J. E., Semenov, A. D., Michaelson, L., Provan, L. S., Snyder, H. R., & Munakata, Y. (2014). Less-structured time in children's daily lives predicts self-directed executive functioning. *Frontiers in Psychology, 5*, 1-16. doi: 10.3389/fpsyg.2014.00593

Brown, S. L. (2008, May). *Play is more than just fun* [Video file]. Retrieved from https://www.ted.com/talks/stuart_brown_says_play_is_more_than_fun_it_s_vital

Brown, S. L. (2014). *Consequences of play deprivation.* Retrieved from http://www.scholarpedia.org/article/Consequences_of_Play_Deprivation

Brown, T. (2008, May). *Tales of creativity and play* [Video file]. Retrieved from https://www.ted.com/talks/tim_brown_on_creativity_and_play

Craft, A. (2011). *Creativity and education futures: Learning in a digital age.* Stoke on Trent, UK: Trentham Books Limited.

de Charms, R. (1968). *Personal causation: The internal affective determinants of behavior.* New York, NY: Academic Press.

Deci, E. L., & Ryan, R. M. (1985). *Intrinsic motivation and self-determination in human behavior.* New York, NY: Plenum Press.

Ekvall, G. (1996). Organizational climate for creativity and innovation. *European Journal of Work and Organizational Psychology, 5*(1), 105-123.

Farenga, P. (2016). *The foundations of unschooling.* Retrieved from https://www.johnholtgws.com/the-foundations-of-unschooling/

Gallup. (2014). *The state of America's schools: The path to winning again in education.* Retrieved from http://www.gallup.com/services/178769/state-america-schools-report.aspx

Gray, P. (2013). *Free to learn: Why unleashing the instinct to play will make our children happier, more self-reliant, and better students for life.* New York, NY: Basic Books.

Gray, P. (2017). *Self-directed education: Unschooling and democratic schooling.* Retrieved from http://education.oxfordre.com/view/10.1093/acrefore/9780190264093.001.0001/acrefore-9780190264093-e-80

Grolnick, W. S., & Ryan, R. M. (1987). Autonomy in children's learning: An experimental and individual difference investigation. *Journal of Personality and Social Psychology, 52(5)*, 890–898.

Hennessey, B. A. (2010). The Creativity-Motivation Connection. In J. C. Kaufman & R. J. Sternberg (Eds.), *The Cambridge handbook of creativity (pp. 342-365)*. Cambridge, UK: Cambridge University Press.

Hennessey, B. A. (2015). If I were Secretary of Education: A focus on intrinsic motivation and creativity in the classroom. *Psychology of Aesthetics, Creativity, and the Arts, 9*(2), 187-192. doi: http://dx.doi.org/10.1037/aca0000012

Kim, K. H. (2011). The creativity crisis: The decrease in creative thinking scores on the Torrance Tests of Creative Thinking. *Creativity Research Journal, 23*(4), 285–295.

Kim, K. H. (2017, April 17). *2017 creativity crisis update: How high-stakes testing stifles innovation.* Retrieved from http://www.creativitypost.com/education/the_2017_creativity_crisis_update_how_high_stakes_testing_has_stifled_innov

Kim, K. H., & Hull, M. F. (2012). Creative personality and anticreative environment for high school dropouts. *Creativity Research Journal, 24*(2-3), 169–176.

Levin, S., & Engel, S. (2016). *A school of our own: The story of the first student-run high school and a new vision for American education.* New York, NY: The New Press.

National Institute for Play. (n.d.). *The opportunities: Education.* Retrieved from http://www.nifplay.org/opportunities/education/

Osborn, A. F. (1953). *Applied imagination: Principles and procedures of creative thinking.* New York, NY: Charles Scribner's Sons.

Phillips, R. (2014). Space for curiosity. *Progress in Human Geography, 38*(4), 493-512.

Puccio, G. J., Mance, M., & Murdock, M. C. (2011). *Creative leadership: Skills that drive change* (2nd ed.). Thousand Oaks, CA: SAGE Publications.

Riley, G. (2015). Differences in competence, autonomy, and relatedness between home-educated and traditionally educated young adults. *International Social Science Review, 90*(2), 1-27.

Ryan, R. M. (1993). Agency and organization: Intrinsic motivation, autonomy and the self in psychological development. In J. Jacobs (Ed.), *Nebraska*

Symposium on Motivation: Vol. 40. Developmental perspectives on motivation (pp. 1–56). Lincoln, NE: University of Nebraska Press.

Ryan, R. M., & Deci, E. L. (2000). Self-determination theory and the facilitation of intrinsic motivation, social development, and well- being. *American Psychologist, 55(1),* 68–78.

Ryan, R. M., & Deci, E. L. (2017). *Self-determination theory: Basic psychological needs in motivation, development, and wellness.* New York, NY: The Guilford Press.

Sawyer, R. K. (2008). Optimising learning: Implications of learning sciences research. In D. Grandrieux & V. Shadoian (Eds.), *Innovating to learn, learning to innovate* (pp. 45-65). Paris, France: OECD Publishing.

Speicher, S. (2017). *The uncomfortable secret to creative success is "disequilibrium".* Retrieved from https://qz.com/1118085/the-uncomfortable-secret-to-creative-success-is-disequilibrium/

Torrance, E. P. (1966). *The Torrance Tests of Creative Thinking–Norms: Technical manual research edition—Verbal tests, Forms A and B—Figural tests, Forms A and B.* Princeton, NJ: Personnel Press.

Torrance, E. P. (1983a). The importance of falling in love with "something." *Creative Child and Adult Quarterly, 8*(2), 72-78.

Torrance, E. P. (1983b). *Manifesto for children.* Athens, GA: Georgia Studies of Creative Behavior and Full Circle Counseling, Inc.

Torrance, E. P. (2002). *The manifesto: A guide to developing a creative career.* Westport, CT: Ablex Publishing.

Waters, L. (2017). *The strength switch: How the new science of strength-based parenting can help your child and your teen to flourish.* New York, NY: Avery.

About the Author

Nicole Colter is a serial entrepreneur and educator who is passionate about Self-Directed Education. She will complete her Master of Science in Creative Studies from the International Center for Studies in Creativity at SUNY Buffalo State in August 2018 and earned a Bachelor of Business Administration in Human Resource Management with a minor in Law from Baruch College.

Nicole is on a mission to disrupt pervasive mindlessness and set people free from self-imposed constraints. She is exploring what might be all the ways to achieve this mission in service of the growing Self-Directed Education movement. Her areas of interest include education practices and environments that create self-directed learners and she is currently intrigued by unschooling, open education, connectivism, and rhizomatic learning. Her other interests include entrepreneurship education, mentoring, community building and cooperative business.

Email: hope@nicolecolter.com
LinkedIn: www.linkedin.com/in/nicolecolter
Twitter: @nicolecolter

CREATIVE PROCESS

How Might Emergent Thinking Bridge the Gap Between Divergent and Convergent Thinking Throughout the Creative Problem Solving Process?

Brian D. Kalina
International Center for Studies in Creativity
SUNY Buffalo State

Abstract

This chapter will explore a stage of thinking in between divergent and convergent thinking, referred to as *emergent thinking,* which might be useful during the Creative Problem Solving (CPS) process. While facilitating teams and individuals through CPS, I have observed that there is a period when ideas are no longer being generated, nor has the selection process begun. The ideas are simply being discussed, explained, explored, and/or played with. As a result, thoughts emerge. This action in and of itself is not exactly divergent because they are not generating new ideas. And while these ideas may be useful, they would fall short of the accepted definition of creativity as they lack novelty. Therefore, an intermediate stage of thinking (emergent thinking) may be called for. This chapter will explore the nature of emergent thinking, the possible guidelines of emergent thinking, how emergent thinking fits within the dynamic balance of divergent and convergent thinking, and how we might facilitate emergent thinking.

How Might Emergent Thinking Bridge the Gap Between Divergent and Convergent Thinking Throughout the Creative Problem Solving Process?

One of the hallmarks of the Creative Problem Solving (CPS) process is the separation of thinking into two distinct types: divergent and convergent thinking (Miller, Vehar, Firestien, Thurber, & Nielsen, 2011). In fact, while CPS has undergone many changes since its conception, this separation has not been altered since the process was first penned in 1953 by Alex Osborn in the book *Applied Imagination*. Puccio, Mance, Switalski, and Reali (2012) expanded on the importance of separating divergent and convergent thinking through their examination of the relationship between divergent and convergent thinking, known as the *dynamic balance of creativity*.

Divergent thinking is all about generating a multitude of ideas, making lists, and conceiving as many options as possible (Parnes, 1992). Osborn (1953) set forth the following guidelines to ensure that proper divergence occurs: defer judgment, build and combine ideas, seek wild ideas, and go for quantity. In contrast, convergent thinking is all about categorizing and clustering those ideas generated in the divergent stage, evaluating them based on pre-determined criteria, and then selecting the key idea(s) or concept(s) to move forward. Convergent thinking has its own set of guidelines: be deliberate, check your objectives, be affirmative, and seek novelty (Miller et al., 2011).

The key to creative thinking is not only to separate divergent and convergent thinking, but to engage in divergent thinking before you engage in convergent thinking, and to employ both types of thinking (in that order) at every stage of the CPS process. In other words, no matter which stage of CPS you are working within—clarify, ideate, develop, or implement—you must diverge first, then converge (Miller et al., 2011).

The question then becomes, is that all there is to it? Based on personal experience and observations while facilitating and working with groups, there seems to be a period during the process when neither divergent nor convergent thinking is taking place. A person tasked with solving a problem (either alone or in a group) is neither generating ideas nor selecting them. Rather it seems there is a period of exploration occurring—a different and unique type of thinking which I will refer to as emergent thinking.

Emergent Thinking Defined

Emergent thinking involves explaining, elaborating, exploring, and mentally experimenting with ideas. The goal is to discover more about the ideas generated in the divergent stage, and/or follow the paths of ideas—the result of which may (or may not) be the realization of a new idea or insight. Simply stated, emergent thinking may be defined as exploring for potential and/or making sense of the ideas that have been generated.

It is true that new ideas often emerge from conceptual combinations, or the fusion of two familiar concepts that result in a new concept (Sawyer, 2012). The point of emergent thinking is to engage in exploration and discussion, but not to judge or select ideas. It is the mental process, not the result, that is the focus. The formation of ideas is the main focus of divergent thinking. Determining how new or how useful those ideas might be falls squarely in the domain of convergent thinking. Therefore, emergent thinking is more than just a subset of divergent thinking or a product of convergent thinking. The main purpose of emergent thinking is to allow for and to set up for incubation.

Emergent thinking differs from incubation in that incubation is a result of emergent thinking, not the other way around. Incubation is mostly concerned with mulling over the discussion and choices in a less deliberate manner. Guilford (1979) defined incubation as

> a period in the behavior of the individual during which there is no apparent activity on his part toward the solution of a problem, but during which or at the end of which there are definite signs of further attempts. (p. 1)

Furthermore, Guilford (1979) credits Poincaré with "the oldest theory of incubation. [It] is an 'unconscious mind' working on the problem after the conscious mind has laid it aside" (p. 1). Simply stated, the mind wanders and follows its course, making connections along the way (Sawyer, 2012). Finally, Parnes (1992) stated that "Incubation is more typically looked upon as something that happens after the deliberate effort stops" (p. 140). As such, incubation is different than emergent thinking because emergent thinking is more active (and deliberate) than incubation.

Examples of emergent thinking, just like divergent and convergent thinking, can be found in every stage of CPS. As a facilitator of CPS sessions, I have observed the process of emergent thinking many times. Phrases that are indicative of emergent thinking are, "That reminds me of..." or, through the use of analogy and metaphor during ideation, "It's like that scene in that movie..." "Did you ever read the book…" or "This reminds me of the way a bird flies or a monkey gathers food…"

Emergent thinking and the conversations associated with it are useful for teams and individuals when solving problems as they allow for ideas to be fully investigated, add context to a possible solution, and can act as a catalyst for new ideas or insights. For example, if a participant in a group has his or her memory jogged by an idea from another participant and then says so aloud, that may in turn lead to yet another new idea. However, the new idea may not have ever been formulated without that connection verbally expressed in the group.

Keeping the Dynamic Balance of Creativity Balanced

Puccio et al. (2012) stated that a balance between divergent and convergent thinking exists throughout the Creative Problem Solving process. So then, what might be the fulcrum in the middle? What is the support point that keeps both divergent and convergent thinking in check? Emergent thinking may be the middle point that indicates whether or not we are over-extending on either of the two sides. If we are too heavy on either divergent or convergent thinking, the question we should ask ourselves becomes, to what degree have we explored the merits of our ideas? Have we been so hyper focused on generating ideas that we have failed, after diverging, to be deliberate in the consideration of what they mean? Conversely, have we been so determined in selecting one solution that we have not given ourselves the opportunity to explore whether or not a few ideas might solve our problem?

The diagram below (Fig. 1) is an illustration of how emergent thinking fits in and may be the missing piece to Puccio et al.'s (2012) *Dynamic Balance of Creativity:*

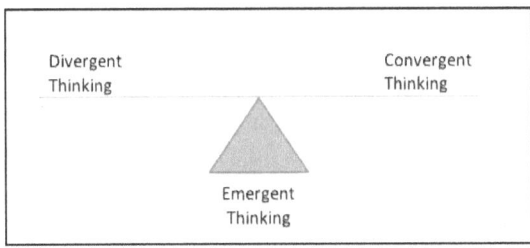

Figure 1. Emergent thinking is the fulcrum between divergent and convergent thinking.

With this model in mind, we can see how emergent thinking is similar to homeostasis in biology. Homeostasis is the body's way of achieving balance. It is the point in which the body finds some kind of resolution before engaging in a new activity. In the case of creative thinking, emergent thinking can be thought of as the brain working towards homeostasis. In other words, the brain is trying to make sense of the ideas vying for its attention, and must attempt to reach a homeostatic state through the form of emergent thinking. Before we can move into convergent thinking, we must take stock of our ideas, contextualize them, and bring order to those ideas generated during divergent thinking.

Hommel (2012) stated, "divergent and convergent thinking not only differs with respect to their computational goals but also seem to rely on different functional and neural mechanisms" (p. 230). In fact, Chermahini and Hommel (2010) went on to say that many authors tend to agree, "that truly creative acts do not reflect the operation of just one process, brain area, or intellectual faculty but, rather, the interplay of multiple cognitive processes and neural networks" (p. 458).

To study activity in the brain, researchers (Chermahini & Hommel, and Dietrich) used the Alternate Uses Task (AUT: Guilford, 1967) and the Remote Associates Task (RAT: Mednick, 1962.) As a result, according to Hommel, (2012) the findings suggest that "There is evidence that divergent-thinking performance relates to the individual dopamine level of participants in the form of an inverted U-shape, with medium levels allowing for the best performance, whereas convergent-thinking performance shows a linear, negative relationship with dopamine levels" (p. 230-231). Therefore, this research would suggest that the brain experiences and reaches a "middle point" when emergent thinking takes place as an individual makes the transition from divergent thinking to convergent thinking.

Emergent Thinking Guidelines

Similar to divergent and convergent thinking, engaging in emergent thinking requires guidelines to be successful. While more research needs to be conducted to validate these guidelines, the following represents a preliminary list: explain and elaborate on your thinking, explore the path, mentally experiment with ideas, and embrace novelty. The questions of how the guidelines might relate and build upon each other, and ultimately help us advance to the next stage of thinking (convergent thinking) were considered while creating these guidelines.

The first guideline, *explain and elaborate on your thinking,* is the foundation of emergent thinking. Ideas generated during divergent thinking are often incomplete and need further explanation. These so called "germs" or "sparks" of ideas can benefit from additional detail and description. Yet elaboration is not always appropriate during the divergent thinking stage because the time and effort it takes to explain an idea would be detrimental to generating a large quantity of ideas—slowing down the process and hampering the ability to seek wild ideas. *Explaining and elaborating on your thinking* (after divergence) is beneficial as it puts ideas into context and may help other participants gain a deeper understanding of an idea before converging on them.

The second guideline, *explore the path,* is important because it prevents us from prematurely evaluating ideas and converging too quickly. It is a natural extension of the first guideline in that it encourages us to make connections and stay open to new ideas. By exploring the path and allowing ideas to take us to new places, we are deliberately engaging in the creative process. Who knows what new paths we will find or what new doors may open for us if we stayed fixed in our thinking? The exploring the path guideline promotes the act of finding novel ways of solving a problem. Once these paths have been investigated and traveled, then we are much better prepared to transition into the convergent thinking stage.

Next, *mentally experiment with ideas*. This guideline is about drawing comparisons, making analogies, and looking for similes and metaphors. The important distinction here is that this guideline is a mental process and not the process of prototyping an idea to look for strengths and weaknesses of a proposed solution. Mentally experimenting with ideas allows for the opportunity of proper incubation to take place before advancing to the convergent stage.

Finally, the *embrace novelty* guideline of emergent thinking is a precursor to the "seek novelty" (Miller et al., 2011) guideline found in convergent thinking. The difference between these two guidelines is the actions surrounding "novelty." In emergent thinking one embraces novelty by keeping an open mind and tolerating ambiguity. In the course of convergent thinking, seeking novelty speaks to the selection of ideas and the importance of choosing an idea that is different than previous solutions to a problem or challenge. Embracing novelty within emergent thinking helps to ensure that we are being deliberate in our pursuit to fulfill the classic definition that creativity is a combination of novelty and usefulness (Stein, 1953).

Facilitating Emergent Thinking

Many of the same behaviors a skilled CPS facilitator would exhibit during divergent and convergent thinking will be present when guiding individuals and teams through the emergent thinking stage. For example, while facilitating divergent and convergent thinking, active listening is a crucial skill (Schwarz, Davidson, Carlson, & McKinney, 2005). The same is true when facilitating emergent thinking. Through the use of open-ended questions, or statement starters such as, "Tell me more about..." "Let's explore that a little further..." "Explain the concept..." proper emergent thinking will naturally follow.

Particular attention must be paid by the facilitator to ensure that conversations are in service of the challenge. Otherwise, these conversations run the risk of becoming meaningless and a waste of time. Participants should not take advantage of the emergent thinking stage and use it as an opportunity to engage in idle chatter or confuse it with discussions that are merely a diversion from the task at hand.

If we refer back to the emergent thinking guidelines, we see that *exploring the path* and *embracing novelty* become equally important for the facilitator. The point here is to ask questions that give more context to the participants' ideas, instead of asking a question to satisfy curiosity or catalyze a completely new and independent thought. If, however, new ideas and thoughts arise from the explanation of the idea, then the facilitator has been successful in enabling both an environment and discussion where new ideas can emerge. The next step, then, is to let the conversation organically continue. In this way, the facilitator is modeling the behavior outlined in the guidelines of *explain and elaborate on your thinking, explore the path, mentally experiment with ideas, and embrace novelty.*

Conclusion

Over the years, the most enduring quality of CPS has been its ability to be true to the idea that creativity is not just novel, but useful as well. In this regard, CPS is a living framework that invites evolution and modification. Therefore, it stands to reason that creativity practitioners will continue to diverge and generate new tools, techniques, and constructs. After doing so, they will converge and select the tools, techniques, and constructs that are most applicable to advancing the practice of creativity.

The concept of emergent thinking has been a product of my studies in creativity and CPS. Through explanation, exploration, and experimentation, and by following the path of creativity and cognition, I believe that I have uncovered this interesting stage of emergent thinking. Simply put, emergent thinking has led to the notion that emergent thinking exists. Perhaps this is the missing step in how we approach ideas and creativity. What might be all the ways we can explore this further?

References

Buzan, T., & Buzan, B. (1993). *The mind map book: How to use radiant thinking to maximize your brain's untapped potential.* London, UK: BBC Books.

Chermahini, S. A., & Hommel, B. (2010). The (b)link between creativity and dopamine:Spontaneous eye blink rates predict and dissociate divergent and convergent thinking. *Cognition, 115*(3), 458-465.

Creative Education Foundation. (2016). *Creative Problem Solving resource guide.* Retrieved from http://www.creativeeducationfoundation.org/wp-content/uploads/2016/06/CPS-Guide_2016-web.pdf

Dietrich, A. (2004). The cognitive neuroscience of creativity. *Psychonomic Bulletin & Review, 11*, 1011–1026.

Gordon, W. J. J. (1961). *Synectics: The development of creative capacity.* New York, NY: Harper.

Guilford, J. P. (1967). *The nature of human intelligence.* New York, NY: McGraw-Hill.

Guilford, J. P. (1979). Some incubated thoughts on incubation. *The Journal of Creative Behavior, 13*(1), 1-8.

Hommel, B. (2012). Convergent and divergent operations in cognitive search. In Todd, P. M., Hills, T. T., & Robbins, T. W. (Eds.), *Cognitive search: Evolution, algorithms, and the brain.* (pp. 221-235). Cambridge, MA: MIT Press.

Mednick, S. (1962). The associative basis of creative problem solving process. *Psychological Review, 69*, 200-232.

Miller, B., Vehar, J., Firestien, R., Thurber, S., & Nielsen, D. (2011). *Creativity unbound: An introduction to creative process* (5th ed.). Evanston, IL: FourSight.

Osborn, A. F. (1953). *Applied imagination.* New York, NY: Charles Scribner's Sons.

Parnes, S. J. (Ed.). (1992). *Source book for creative problem solving: A fifty year digest of proven innovation processes.* Amherst, MA: Creative Education Foundation Press.

Puccio, G. J., Mance, M., Barbero Switalski, L., & Reali, P. D. (2012). Creativity rising: Creative thinking and creative problem solving in the 21st century. Buffalo, NY: ICSC Press.

Puccio, G. J., Mance, M., & Murdock, M. C. (2011). *Creative leadership: Skills that drive change* (2nd ed.). Thousand Oaks, CA: SAGE Publications.

Puccio, G. J., Murdock, M. C., & Mance, M. (2005). Current developments in creative problem solving for organizations: A focus on thinking skills and styles. *The Korean Journal of Thinking and Problem Solving, 15*(2), 43-76.

Sawyer, R. K. (2012). *Explaining creativity: The science of human innovation* (2nd ed.). New York, NY: Oxford University Press.

Schwarz, R. M., Davidson, A., Carlson, P., & McKinney, S. (2005). *The skilled facilitator fieldbook: Tips, tools, and tested methods for consultants, facilitators, managers, trainers, and coaches.* San Francisco, CA: Jossey-Bass.

Stein, M. I. (1953). Creativity and culture. *The Journal of Psychology, 36*(2), 311-322.

Tassoul, M., & Buijs, J. (2007). Clustering: An essential step from diverging to converging. *Creativity and Innovation Management, 16*(1), 16-26.

About the Author

With over 20 years of experience in advertising, Brian has devoted his professional career to generating big ideas based on true human insights. As a Creative Director, Brian has produced award winning work for globally recognized brands at agencies such as DDB New York, Ogilvy, and FCB Health. He has also functioned as a Strategic Planning Director utilizing his deep creative abilities to help amplify the strategic thinking process aimed at solving business issues and implementing change.

Brian is a trained facilitator in both Creative Problem Solving and LEGO® SERIOUS PLAY® methodologies and regularly attends the Creative Problem Solving Institute (CPSI). Brian has successfully led hundreds of Ideation sessions, guiding teams through the creative problem solving process to arrive at various outcomes including: positioning, competitive analysis and simulations, tactic and campaign creation, and team building. When Brian is not at home in NJ with his wife, two children, and a dog named Reggie, you will find him studying at the International Center for Studies in Creativity at SUNY Buffalo State, delving deeper into a wide variety of facilitation and strategic thinking methodologies and creative theory such as, Six Thinking Hats, Human Centered Design, Service Design, Business Model Generation, and many others.

What Does It Take to Tolerate Ambiguity? A Search Into Love, Happiness, and Balance

Anneke Veenendaal-de Kort
International Center for Studies in Creativity
SUNY Buffalo State

Abstract

This paper explores three concepts—falling in love with something, happiness, and balancing the familiar and the unknown—and their relations to the creativity skill tolerating ambiguity. This literature review reveals that all three factors can increase tolerance for ambiguity. The paper reflects on different sources that demonstrate that falling in love with something makes people more courageous and action-oriented and helps them to open up and tolerate ambiguity. Further insight is provided on the effect happiness has on one's tolerance for ambiguity. And it is concluded that a good balance between the familiar and the element of surprise enhances tolerance for ambiguity (Luna & Renninger, 2015).

What Does It Take to Tolerate Ambiguity? A Search Into Love, Happiness, and Balance

As a communications consultant who facilitates organizational change, I see more and more companies are gaining the awareness that creativity is important. Change is happening so fast that organizations cannot fall back on solutions from the past. They are increasingly confronted with situations that haven't occurred before and demand new thinking. I have spent the past ten years wondering and researching the effective development of creativity in different organizations. Many organizations talk about the need for creativity rather than developing it within their own walls. Their attention is taken up by delivering on and improving their core business model. Many of the changes that organizations go through are based on "need to have" and not "nice to have," so organizational leaders are pressured to focus on 'more important' things before tackling creativity.

Creativity could greatly help organizations to face their future challenges, but developing creativity takes a lot of time and effort. It's not just a matter of learning tools that can help individuals generate, select, develop, and implement ideas. As Puccio (2017) discussed in a video interview, it takes a creative mindset, skillset, and toolset.

I have observed that most of the attention of organizations attempting to develop their internal creativity is focused on the creative toolset, and is usually facilitated by external creativity experts, often resulting in only a few sustainable results within the organization itself. Organizations would benefit from giving more attention to the creative mindset and skillset of their people as well. In order to be creative, it is vital to learn how to think creatively, and thinking interacts with our affective skills (attitudes, feelings, and emotions). The Creative Problem Solving process (CPS) as described in the book *Creative Leadership: Skills That Drive Change* (Puccio, Mance, & Murdock, 2011) beautifully links thinking skills to affective skills and demonstrates how important it is to connect thinking and feeling in order to get into action. "Without an affective domain to partner with the cognitive domain, learning and understanding would not likely go beyond simple transmittal of information" (Puccio et al. 2011, p. 62).

Learning How to Tolerate Ambiguity

The different phases of the CPS process require different affective skills (Puccio et al., 2011). The affective skills are "powerful partners with cognitive skills" (Murdock, Burnett, & Mance, 2008, p.1). Puccio et al. (2011) identified three overarching affective skills that are a necessary part of their Thinking Skills Model (TSM): openness to novelty, tolerance for complexity, and tolerance for ambiguity. Managing these three major emotional competencies forms a strong foundation for creativity.

To challenge myself, I reflected on the quality of my own basic affective skillset. Openness to novelty is in my core, as is tolerance for complexity. However, I realized that I struggle with tolerance for ambiguity: there are times where I am quite comfortable not knowing the outcomes, yet there are other times where I am very uncomfortable when I am unsure about what the future brings. When ambiguity brings discomfort, it can be so overwhelming that I do not dare to make any decisions or take actions. So what does it take to tolerate ambiguity?

Puccio et al. (2011) defined tolerating ambiguity as "being able to deal with uncertainty and to avoid leaping to conclusions" (p. 64). Murdock et al. (2008) encouraged readers to practice tolerance for ambiguity by focusing on the present moment, appreciating the benefits of keeping things ambiguous, and slowing down before responding (p. 14). These definitions and tips led me to the question: Why are some people better able to tolerate ambiguity than others?

Definitions of Tolerance (for Ambiguity)

Tolerance from a biological perspective is "the ability of an organism to withstand extreme variations in environmental conditions" (Hine & Martin, 2015, p. 592). This definition is perfectly applicable for organizations or individuals who need to grow. The more flexible you are to adapt to any changes around you, the better chances you have to withstand those changes and survive. Like plants needing to stand strong in the soil in order to be able to connect to the nutrition to grow, people and organizations need to stand strong on the foundation from which they will grow. And like plants, they must be flexible: if you tighten all your muscles and stand rigidly, you can be easily pushed over. But when you manage to flex your muscles, you are more able to adapt and find where the 'good nutrition' is. Luna and Renninger (2015) said it best:

> If Darwin were around he'd stroke his beard and say: 'What you've got here, folks, is the case of a changing ecosystem.' When a climate transforms from stormy to dry, only the finches with the proper ad-

aptations—a certain beak shape—are able to obtain food and thus survive. (p. 35)

Now let's shift from examining *tolerance* to understanding *tolerance for ambiguity*. Chandler and Munday (2016) define tolerance for ambiguity as being comfortable with situations or stimuli that lack a single clear and regular pattern or an obviously correct interpretation. Intolerant people tend to transform irregularities into standard forms more than others: they look for structure and when it's not there, they create it. Context plays an important role. Chandler and Munday (2016) stated that, "Contexts in which rational analysis has a high status (such as scientific research) tend to discourage ambiguity; contexts in which individual interpretation is prominent (such as the arts) tend to show more acceptance of it" (p. 435).

I feel that if you wish to increase creativity in your organization, it is vital that you create an environment where people feel that ambiguity is accepted. It may be helpful for people to accept ambiguity when they work in an environment where the vulnerability to do so is demonstrated by leadership. I have noticed a strong desire from those in leadership positions to communicate clear solutions and concrete knowledge and approaches; not many managers feel comfortable presenting ideas to the rest of the organization before all is clear and all solutions have been designed. Based on these observations, I was able to develop my first piece of advice to organizations regarding tolerating ambiguity: When you want your people to develop a creative mindset, you should set the example and show that you are open to and can cope with uncertainty. Oftentimes it is just as important to share what you don't know as it is to share what you know. Be open to the fact that you do not know what the future holds and what impact it will have on the organization and the people in it. The more transparent you are about living in this uncertain state together, the more you can exercise tolerance and develop the creative climate in your organization.

The Perception of Tolerance

Based on my own experiences, when I compare situations where I am good at tolerating ambiguity to situations where I'm not, I see three important factors that play a role. The first is loving what I do. When I work on something that I've fallen in love with, there is nothing that can stop me, no insecurities that can take me away from my drive. I cannot stop coming up with more interesting and surprising ideas to develop what I'm working on.

The second aspect that I recently realized plays a crucial role is happiness. When I'm emotionally in a good place, I can move mountains. Creating becomes my middle name. I have so much energy and flow that I needn't be afraid of ambiguity. I know that I am flexible enough to deal with any uncertainty because I am capable of coming up with different options. In these situations, ambiguity is not just okay, it's at the heart of the flexibility and surprise I desire to keep feeling alive and not get bored.

Last, I need balance. I am better able to bear uncertainties in one area when I can trust on certainties in another. When I need to do something new in my field of expertise, I'm comfortable experimenting because I know my expertise will get me through it. If I have to do something new within a related field, I can usually tolerate that ambiguity because I already have a basic understanding of similar challenges in my field. When I am experiencing something completely new, I try to use what is familiar to me in order to cope. In balancing the familiar with the unknown, is it knowledge that gives me confidence. Too much uncertainty will make me freeze, so I need to balance the familiar and the unknown. The question now becomes: Are my experiences in line with what research says? Have I found the recipe for developing a tolerance for ambiguity?

In the following sections, I will dig deeper into the research about what I frame as my three potential tolerance-factors: falling in love with something, happiness, and balancing the familiar and the unknown.

Falling in Love with Something

The examples that stand out for me regarding my own tolerance for ambiguity are the times where I've taken the biggest risks and given up certainty in my life. Several years ago I gave up a great job to start my own company. The decision to do this was pretty much made overnight because I had an idea that I fell in love with. Then, after a couple of years as an entrepreneur, I decided to leave my solid client base behind and take time off to write a book. I was uncertain if it would be successful, uncertain if I would be making enough money, uncertain that doors would reopen with past clients when I was ready to come back. Still, none of this ever stopped me. I had an idea that I loved, and I dug into it. The interesting fact is that it has been exactly these times that I have been most successful. In these cases, my creativity has flowed and the results were exciting for me.

Trusting and Loving Yourself

So what does science teach us that could make love a contributing factor to tolerance for ambiguity? When you fall in love, dopamine, a neurotransmitter that controls the brain's reward and pleasure centers, is released. Since falling in love gives your brain its own rewards, you become less dependent on extrinsic rewards that are more difficult to control (Kim, 2017). Research from Amabile (1997) on the effect of intrinsic motivation on creativity showed that the more interested people were in their tasks (loving what they did), the more creative their results. In this study, the group that got to perform the task they loved most turned out the most creative products, whereas the group that had to perform a task in order to get a bonus produced much less creative outputs (Amabile, 1997). Doing what you love reduces concern for social approval (Barron, 1955), and therefore increases your tolerance for ambiguity in not knowing how others might react or respond.

According to Torrance (2002), falling in love with something also makes us action-oriented. It gives us the courage and the will to take important initiatives and move forward to new solutions and achievements (Torrance, 2002). It helps a great deal when you fall in love with something at an early age and persist throughout your life: Torrance (1980) found strong evidence for this in his 22-year longitudinal study of elementary school children. The children who stuck to their dreams and who were fortunate to have teachers, parents, and mentors who understood, respected, and supported the things they were in love with were ultimately the most motivated to pursue their dreams (Torrance, 1980). This demonstrates that falling in love is just a first step. I believe it takes more to move past infatuation. Whether you fall in love with something or you fall in love with someone, falling in love is the easy and fun bit. Committing to and working for a relationship (or project) can be stressful and aggravating, so it is helpful to have a follow-up strategy to ensure you are able to continue tolerating ambiguity for the longer term.

Happiness

When I'm in a good mood, I'm energized and open to trying and discovering new things. I don't need certainties when my curiosity is flowing. My good mood doesn't just make me tolerant of ambiguity, it makes me look for ambiguity, because it makes me feel alive to discover new things and to be surprised along the way – just like when I started writing this paper. I was genuinely curious to find out more about tolerance for ambiguity, and I fed my inspiration through my own curiosity. I didn't need answers. I was open to generating more questions and living in the uncertainty of not knowing the answers.

Then, in the middle of this project, I was told that my dad was terminally ill. This news killed my flow instantly. I spent days and nights pushing myself to come up with a good set-up for my paper, and I couldn't do it. The harder I pushed, the more uncertain I became. And this was a different kind of uncertain. This was the kind that stopped me from realizing my dreams, where the previous kind of uncertainty was the kind that inspired my curiosity and attention. I realized this was an important insight in my search for the ambiguity tolerance factors. For me, having the ability to be open to uncertainty and being led by curiosity requires happiness. I am convinced that happiness is the longer-term strategy to tolerating ambiguity after the love begins to wear off.

Self-actualized People Embrace the Unknown

My belief that happiness is an important ingredient to tolerating ambiguity is supported by Maslow's (1987) theory of self-actualization, which stated that self-actualized people embrace the unknown and the ambiguous. "They are not threatened or afraid of it; instead, they accept it, are comfortable with it and are often attracted by it. They do not cling to the familiar" (Sze, 2015, para. 4). Self-actualization arises when people are truly happy (Sullivan, 2009). So what does it take to be truly happy?

Seligman and Royzman (2003) state different types of traditional theories of happiness: Hedonism, Desire, and Objective List. These theories lead to different ways of being happy in life. "The Pleasant Life is about happiness in Hedonism's sense. The Good Life is about happiness in Desire's sense, and the Meaningful Life is about happiness in Objective List's sense" (Seligman & Royzman, 2003, para. 11).

According to Weijers (2017), Hedonia refers to the instant pleasure you can experience from, for example, eating chocolate, bungee jumping, or going wild at a dance party. A hedonist, therefore, "seeks pleasure and avoids pain" (Ben-Shahar, 2007, p. 20). This pleasant life is experienced in the here and now. Seligman (2002) provided good advice on how people can enhance their pleasures through habituation (i.e., spreading out the events that produce pleasure enough to generate a craving), savoring (i.e., indulging the senses), and mindfulness (i.e., becoming acutely aware of the surrounding).

The good life refers to getting what you want. "The fulfillment of a desire contributes to one's happiness regardless of the amount of pleasure (or displeasure)" (Seligman & Royzman, 2003, para. 6). Scientists agree that chasing after pleasure and desire isn't enough to make people happier; bringing meaning to the life of others and the world around us is what brings people true and authentic happiness, or a full life (Seligman & Royzman, 2003).

The Chicken or the Egg?

I began to wonder whether people who are tolerant of ambiguity are happier, or happier people are more tolerant of ambiguity. I did not find any research on tolerance for ambiguity that looked specifically at this question, but Inglehart, Foa, Peterson, and Welzel's 2008 data analysis found that there is a relationship between tolerance to ambiguity and happiness in general, which gives food for thought. Among other things, an increased tolerance (for ambiguity or otherwise) is responsible for a considerable rise in overall world happiness (Mabe, 2008). The World Values Survey shows that when we feel less threatened, we are more tolerant, which makes us happier (Mabe, 2008). Budner (1962) stated that those who perceive ambiguous situations as threatening experience negative feelings, such as anxiety, and may react behaviorally with strategies to avoid or reduce the discomfort.

This leads me to the conclusion that tolerance, in general, is the cause, and happiness is the consequence. Such a conclusion is confirmed by others' strategies to increase happiness, such as Seligman's PERMA (2011) and McDonough's whole-being theory of SPIRE (2015), where resilience plays an important role in happiness. Feeling all our emotions, positive as well as negative, leads us to resilience (McDonough, 2015). We humans suffer from negativity-bias, meaning we tend to focus on what's broken or not working (McDonough, 2015). Hanson (n.d.) stated, "In effect the brain is like Velcro for negative experiences, but Teflon for positive ones" (para. 5).

Examples in creative history show that positive environments or situations lead to more creativity, such as mathematician Henri Poincare, who experienced his creative breakthroughs while on vacation, or Mozart, who claimed that pleasant moods were most conducive to his creativity:

> When I am, as it were, completely myself, entirely alone, and of good cheer-say, traveling in a carriage, or walking after a good meal, or during the night when I cannot sleep; it is on such occasions that my ideas flow best and most abundantly. (as cited in Vernon, 1970, p. 55)

These examples illustrate the benefits of letting go of some of the control that many of us tend to cling on to. They show that breaking loose from a location or situation that is familiar to us can have a positive effect on creativity and happiness.

However, "it is not the perfectly planned and controlled moments that make us the happiest. It's the surprising ones" (Luna & Renninger, 2015, p. xx). This statement not only illustrates the importance of happiness, but shows us why we must seek to balance the familiar with the unknown.

Balancing the Familiar and the Unknown

I'm much better at tolerating the unfamiliar when I approach a challenge or task in the field of communications, where I've spent my entire career, than when I am participating in, for example, a creativity training or situation where I must use skills that I acquired later in my professional life. When I deliver a training to a group, I sometimes prepare for days. I know that trainings never go as planned, but I have learned that this extensive preparation makes me so comfortable that it allows me the flexibility to be spontaneous. Apparently, I need the certainty of confidence to guard myself against the uncertainty. Csikszentmihalyi (1996) shared that highly creative people follow patterns and standardize many aspects of life, like wearing the same clothes every day (like Steve Jobs and his black turtlenecks), so that they have room for new ideas and experiences.

Luna and Renninger (2015) referred to this as a Surprise Seesaw – the balance of the familiar and surprise. "When there is plenty of certainty on our Surprise Seesaw, we welcome dipping into unpredictability" (Luna & Renninger, 2015, p. 48). In other words, we should be able to trust what we know and be delighted with situations which are new to us. Luna and Renninger (2015) stated, "trust is a psychological safety net that allows us to let go, whether it's letting go of the trapeze bar to fling your body through the air or letting go of certainty to embrace the unpredictable" (p. 47). The authors shared three strategies to help embrace the unpredictable:

1. Resilience is the internal sense of certainty we need in order to let surprise in,

2. We need to reframe vulnerability from weak to open, and

3. We need to become skilled at not knowing (Luna & Renninger, 2015).

According to Luna and Renninger (2015), too much predictability makes us so bored that we lose attention, allowing predictable ideas to slip by us without our notice. When something novel happens (a surprise), we freeze, giving it extra attention, but when something is too new and unpredictable, we may not pay attention simply because we cannot put it into one of our existing frames (Luna & Renninger, 2015). If it is too different from our expectations, we ignore it.

Luna and Renninger (2015) researched couples to find the ultimate balance between security and excitement. They found that in order to be playful and confident in relationships, humans need to feel safe and accepted, which is increasingly likely as we get to know our partners better (Luna & Renninger, 2015). At the same time, we are most attracted to the people that are opposite to us—the unknown excites us. According to the authors, "this is likely caused by a dance between dopamine and oxytocin. Dopamine is linked with desire and oxytocin is called the cuddle drug" (Luna & Renninger, 2015, p. 177).

Conclusions and Next Steps

I began writing this paper around the question, What does it take to tolerate ambiguity? I realize now that I didn't just select a big question, I selected an enormous question. There are so many aspects to look at in addition to the three I chose: falling in love with something, happiness, and the balance between the familiar and the new. While I feel that these three concepts were confirmed by the literature I studied to positively impact tolerance for ambiguity, there are more angles to research.

Falling in love with something can help you accept uncertainty and be more independent of others (Kim, 2017; Torrance, 2002). Some may call it the lack of social approval (Barron, 1955) while others focus on intrinsic motivation (Amabile, 1997), and still others link it to the release of dopamine (Kim, 2017). But regardless of the reasoning, it is clear that being true to yourself can help you tolerate ambiguity and many believe that the ability to tolerate ambiguity increases one's happiness.

Overall I have to conclude that, apart from Luna and Renninger's (2015) spot-on information on tolerating ambiguity, most of the findings for this paper are rather indirect. To gain deeper insight into what effects love and happiness have on tolerating ambiguity, the field requires more empirical research.

My review of the literature clearly leads me to the conclusion that interpersonal factors, such as passion, happiness, and balancing the known and the unfamiliar help a great deal in tolerating ambiguity. However, the environment is important too, and I feel more research is needed to have better insight into what environmental aspects can increase one's tolerance for ambiguity. I began this literature review because I wanted to find ways to help develop organizational creativity. I need to do more research, specifically focusing on organizations, in order to gain better insight into the effects of promoting and facilitating tolerating ambiguity in organizations.

I scratched the surface of three aspects that I find highly interesting. It has provided me a good starting point for further research and activities. I will come up with more related questions, conduct interviews, and review further literature to get more answers, which will ultimately support my end goal: to come up with creative communications strategies that will help organizational creativity increase, due to an increased tolerance for ambiguity.

References

Amabile, T. M. (1997). Motivating creativity in organizations: On doing what you love and loving what you do. *California Management Review, 40*(1), 39-58.

Barron, F. (1955). The disposition toward originality. *The Journal of Abnormal and Social Psychology, 51*(3), 478-485.

Ben-Shahar, T. (2007). *Happier: Learn the secrets to daily joy and lasting fulfillment.* New York, NY: McGraw-Hill.

Budner, S. N. Y. (1962). Intolerance of ambiguity as a personality variable. *Journal of Personality, 30*(1), 29-50. doi: 10.1111/j1467-6494.1962.tb02303.x

Chandler, D., & Munday, R. (2016). *A dictionary of media and communications* (2nd ed.). Oxford, UK: Oxford University Press. doi: 10.1093/acref/9780191800986.001.0001

Csikszentmihalyi, M. (1996). *Creativity: Flow and the psychology of discovery and invention.* New York: NY: HarperCollins.

Hanson, R. (n.d.). Take in the good. [Blog post]. Retrieved from http://www.rickhanson.net/take-in-the-good/

Hine, R. S., & Martin, E. (Eds.). (2015). *A dictionary of biology* (7th ed.). Oxford, UK: Oxford University Press. doi: 10.1093/acref/9780199204625.001.0001

Inglehart, R., Foa, R., Peterson, C., & Welzel, C. (2008). Development, freedom, and rising happiness: A global perspective (1981-2007). *Perspectives on Psychological Science, 3*(4), 264-285.

Kim, S. (2017, February 7). The psychology of falling in love. *University Wire.* Retrieved from http://proxy.buffalostate.edu:2048/login?url=https://search-proquest-com.proxy.buffalostate.edu/docview/1865642013

Luna, T., & Renninger, L. (2015). *Surprise: Embrace the unpredictable and engineer the unexpected.* New York, NY: Perigee.

Mabe, M. (2008, August 20). Survey says: People are happier. [Blog post]. Retrieved from https://www.bloomberg.com/news/articles/2008-08-20/survey-says-people-are-happierbusinessweek-business-news-stock-market-and-financial-advice

Maslow, A. H. (1987). *Motivation and personality* (3rd ed.). R. Frager, J. Fadiman, C. McReynolds, & R. Cox (Eds.). New York, NY: Harper and Row.

McDonough, M. (2015). *Whole-person happiness: A mini workbook on SPIRE: The five dimensions of well-being.* Retrieved from http://wholebeinginstitute.com/wp-content/uploads/Whole-Person-Happiness-a-mini-workbook-3.pdf

Puccio, G. (2017). *What is the content of this Master program?* [Video file]. Retrieved from http://masterchangeskills.eu/learnfromothers/videos/videos-distance-masters-program-in-europe/

Puccio, G. J., Mance, M., & Murdock, M. (2011). *Creative leadership: Skills that drive change* (2nd ed.). Thousand Oaks, CA: SAGE Publications.

Seligman, M. E. P. (2002). *Authentic happiness: Using the new positive psychology to realize your potential for lasting fulfillment.* New York, NY: The Free Press.

Seligman, M. E. P. (2011, April). *Happiness is not enough.* Retrieved from https://www.authentichappiness.sas.upenn.edu/newsletters/flourishnewsletters/newtheory

Seligman, M. E. P., & Royzman, E. (2003, July). *Happiness: The three traditional theories.* Retrieved from https://www.authentichappiness.sas.upenn.edu/newsletters/authentichappiness/happiness

Sullivan, E. (2009). Self-actualization. In B. Kerr (Ed.), *Encyclopedia of giftedness, creativity, and talent* (pp. 791-792). Thousand Oaks, CA: SAGE Publications.

Sze, D. (2015, July 21). *Maslow: The 12 characteristics of a self-actualized person.* Retrieved from http://www.huffingtonpost.com/david-sze/maslow-the-12-characteris_b_7836836.html

Torrance. E. P. (1980). Growing up creatively gifted: A 22-year longitudinal study. *Creative Child and Adult Quarterly, 5*(3), 148-158.

Torrance, E. P. (2002). *The manifesto. A guide to developing a creative career.* Westport, CT: Ablex Publishing.

Weijers, G. (2017). *Boekje waar je blij van wordt.* Culemborg, The Netherlands: Anderz.

About the Author

Anneke Veenendaal-de Kort is a communications consultant who combines creative communications with creative leadership to activate change in organizations from top to bottom and bottom to top. She starts change movements in her client organizations through the design of games, collaboration platforms, visualizations and co-creation sessions. She holds an MSc in Communications from Tilburg University in The Netherlands and an MSc in Creative Studies from SUNY Buffalo State. Anneke is a certified FourSight facilitator. She has been involved in setting-up the marketing and communications of the Master's Program in Creativity and Change Leadership in Europe.

Anneke is the author of a management cookbook filled with recipes for successful change. She has been on a creativity journey for ten years in which she moved from the development of creative thinking skills training, to creative leadership, to the science behind creativity to arrive at her creativity paradise of a creative mindset. For her Master's Project, she designed surprise concepts that aimed to increase people's openness to experience and their tolerance for ambiguity. Anneke is a master in adding surprise and disorder to environments where structure is overrated and openness overlooked.

Email: anneke@zincommunicatie.com
Twitter: @AnnekeZin
Website: www.zincommunicatie.com

CREATIVITY
& LIFE CIRCUMSTANCE

What Impact Does Multiple Sclerosis Have on the Ability to Engage in Creativity?

Danielle Myers
International Center for Studies in Creativity
SUNY Buffalo State

Abstract

This paper explores the impact multiple sclerosis has on a person's ability to learn and engage in creativity. Examining the physical symptoms will help to determine whether or not brain deficiencies can have an impact on learning creativity. Beyond the physical examination, social constructs and personal behaviors are analyzed for their role as impactful influencers. Further neurological research would be beneficial in providing more information on physical limitations and any relationship to creativity. The conclusion proposes that, while some insurmountable limitations exist within the brain that can prevent the ability to learn creativity, it is the consequence of social stigmas which has the greatest impact on creativity suppression.

What Impact Does Multiple Sclerosis Have on the Ability to Engage in Creativity?

2013 was the year when I left my body and entered the realm of never-ending uncertainty. That year, I was ambushed by double vision, which led to a four-day hospital stay and a doctor's release on the premise of "possibility." What I thought was a change in prescription became a black wave that engulfed my body and soul. *What will my quality of life become? What happens when you no longer have control of your own body?* At the age of 24, I was diagnosed with multiple sclerosis.

Multiple sclerosis (MS) is an incurable neurological disease that affects physical, psychological, and social health and well-being (Compston & Coles, 2002). With an unidentifiable origin and an unpredictable future, it is no wonder that MS patients experience an unenviable degree of frustration, which I have come to learn first-hand through my own experience and group therapy meetings. Patients' needs often change during the course of their disease and demand routine adjustments. Treatments are available, but there is little to no evidence that the treatment is working. Success is rated on the number of reoccurring episodes and their severity (Lohne, Aasgaard, Caspari, Slettebo, & Naden, 2010). When an individual's neurological system has been compromised, how does that affect their ability to learn creativity, and what can be done to render resolution?

Symptoms and Stigmas of Multiple Sclerosis

The behavior behind MS can be likened to internal melee. The immune system views the central nervous system as a threat and attacks its communication bases (nerve fibers). The myelin sheath, which is a layer of fatty tissue around the nerves, protects the nerve fibers to ensure communication is not lost throughout the brain and spinal cord. The scar tissue that forms over the destroyed myelin sheath causes a communication interference throughout the body (Falvo, 2009). This interference translates into episodes of relapses and recovery. Episodes are unpredictable in their degree of intensity and in the areas they affect throughout the body. Some episodes may result in a permanent deficiency (Compston et al., 2002).

Since episodes vary in location, it is important to note that no areas are prohibited. MS affects one's physical, cognitive, and psychological state. It is not an apparent disease, which can be problematic because when you do not look ill, it can be difficult for others to believe that you are ill. The most notable symptoms are impaired mobility, including paralysis, muscle weakness, spasticity (muscle spasms), and ataxia (lack of coordination) (Hunt, Nikopoulou-Smyrni, & Reynolds, 2014). Visual impairment is another defining symptom of MS, typically expressed as optic neuritis (temporary blindness), diplopia (double vision), and/or vertigo (Marrie, Cutter, & Tyry, 2011). Nearly all affected by MS frequently experience some degree of fatigue (Hunt et al., 2014).

Cognitive and psychological symptoms are the least obvious. Memory impairment (acute forgetfulness), reduced alertness/concentration, and increased feelings of anxiety and depression are common symptoms that require an additional set of rehabilitation methods (Koch, Rumrill, Roessler, & Fitzgerald, 2001).

From a social perspective, stigmas and a lack of opportunity for creative expression prevent creativity from reaching those to whom it could be most beneficial. The most prevalent example of this is in the workplace. Within a decade of initial diagnosis, nearly half of MS patients will become unemployed (Feys et al., 2016). Since most individuals with MS are unaware of their rights against discrimination, employers tend to use this to their advantage (River et al., 2017). The perception of MS employees/coworkers as "dirty workers" (unclean, shameful, offensive) is also commonplace (Vickers, 2015). Most of the time MS workers expel precious energy trying to rationalize their "dirtiness" and apologize for the way that they are, in order to be accepted (Vickers, 2015). This workplace disadvantage leads to increased levels of poverty, social exclusion, and dependence on social security. The high unemployment rate seen in the MS community is not a result of disability issues, but rather it is the result of employers who simply do not want them (Mechsner, 2004). These financial constraints prevent patients from being able to afford assistive technology that can advance creative learning and allow for participation in creative community classes (Adams, 2003).

Multiple Sclerosis' Impact on Creative Learning

MS impacts learning ability, not only because of its physical and cognitive limitations, but as a result of social stigmas and personal attitudes. Loss of autonomy, self-esteem, dignity, and social roles, along with coping with the disease itself, discourage activity and the interest in developing new habits (Kelly, Cudney, & Weinert, 2012). These factors contribute to an unrealized creative potential.

Symptomatically, fatigue and decreased mobility have the greatest impact on active participation (Smith, 2017). In fact, many venues are not wheelchair accessible (River, Thakoordin, & Billing, 2017). Until recently, it was under medical advisement that active participation in physical activities be strictly avoided (Feys, Giovannoni, Dijsselbloem, Centonze, & Eelen, 2016). The rationale being that people with MS would preserve what little energy they may have and allow that energy to be directed towards daily living chores, not expending it on extracurricular activity. The stress of fatigue, immobility, and medical misinformation prevents patients from participating in physical activities especially if the activity takes place outside of the patient's home.

Atrophy in the corpus callosum, the part of the brain that connects the brain's left and right hemispheres, allowing them to communicate, leads to cognitive impairment. This has been documented in a study using the Thematic Apperception Test (Brown, Paul, Symington, & Dietrich, 2005; Lewis, 1979; Paul, Schieffer, & Brown, 2004). Impairments noted in this study included lack of originality, lack of elaboration, impairments in story logic, social understanding, deficits in narrative humor, and possible impacted divergent thinking (Brown et. al., 2005; Lewis, 1979; Paul et. al., 2004). Myelinated axons, also referred to as protected nerve fibers, in the brain facilitate inter- and intra-hemispheric communication, and both types are essential for creativity. If this area becomes atrophied, this could be devastating for creative growth (Heilman, 2005).

While a significant and important element, affective factors are not the only reason for creativity resistance. Individuals with MS must also play an active role and adjust their attitude towards the disease. They must be conscious enough about their limitations and curious enough to figure out how to work within these constraints, while also reframing their definition of constraint. Additionally, they must have the motivation and a willingness to learn, which can be challenging considering the propensity towards depression, anxiety, and fatigue (Vrkljan & Miller-Polgar, 2001).

Creativity's Impact on Multiple Sclerosis

Creativity's relationship with MS falls into two domains: activity & attitude. Activity is the physical application and attitude is the individual's approach towards creative learning. It is important to have activities from which to learn, but it is perhaps more important to have the motivation to do so. If individuals with MS can discern motivational resolve, then they can begin to achieve goals of need fulfillment (belongingness, esteem, socializing, personal development, and personal safety) (Doward, McKenna, Meads, Twiss, & Eckert, 2009).

Creative activity improves one's ability to cope while increasing the sense of well-being (Kelly et al., 2012). Creative activity in this context refers to any activity that uses a creative approach to achieve better health practices (Kelly et al., 2012). Despite it being discouraged by health care providers for many years, exercise is now one of the most promoted activities in which an individual with MS can take part, and for this reason, is considered a top creative activity. During exercise, the body's cortisol levels increase, helping with energy levels, heightened memory functions, and lower sensitivity to pain (Powers, Dodd, & Noland, 2005). One study found that improvements in upper limb function following intensive exercise were associated with the preservation of the corpus callosum, suggesting that exercise has neuroprotective qualities (Feys et al., 2016). Physical educators can teach movement strategies in the event the body is not cooperating, making it so the individual has movement options (Olenik, 2006). Another example of a creative activity is to attend creative classes which offer social camaraderie and opportunities for learning and development (Hunt et al., 2014). Creative classes may include activities such as gardening, drama, and creative writing. Online tutorials and forums now allow engagement in classes from home, and eliminate concerns regarding accessibility or symptom disruption (Hunt et al, 2014).

Adopting creativity techniques is crucial during the period following diagnosis, since the disease creates circumstances where new interpretations are needed (Vickers, 2011). The ability to reframe problems, analyze situations from various perspectives, make connections, and even collaborate, are ways in which individuals with MS can thrive when managing the disease (River et al., 2017). Creativity is flexible, adaptable, playful and entirely voluntary. More importantly, creativity is without judgment, which is perhaps the most appealing aspect for people with MS. People treat you differently when you have a disease, especially when the disease is indiscernible. This may lead to a perpetual sense of aloneness and lack of relatability, both of which I have come to know. Learning how to be creative provides a way of communicating these emotions in a way that is constructive and therapeutic.

Current Work to Bridge the Creative Divide

Since there is not a cure for this disease, nor a treatment that can reverse its damaging effects, much of the contemporary work on MS revolves around assisting the current and future self.

Exercise. The closest treatment option to result in symptomatic improvement is exercise (Feys et al., 2016). Although exercise is not a conventional medicine, it is considered a complementary therapy, and in our case, a creative activity.

Exercise intervention/community exercise programs are now on the rise, with some focusing on the patient's interests, abilities, and needs.(Olenik, 2006). The PACE (Physical Activity, Creativity, & Evaluation) model is a program that connects medical experts and exercise physiologists to a MS patient to discuss the benefits of an active lifestyle and prevention of progressive conditions that come from being inactive (Olenik, 2006). Blue Prescription, based in New Zealand, is a behavioral exercise therapy model that encourages exercise adherence through a trusted support system created by the individual rather than medical placement (Olenik, 2006). Oregon State University: Corvallis has an MS Exercise Program which assists individuals with obtaining instruction and encouragement to initiate and sustain an exercise protocol (Olenik, 2006). These programs not only encourage physical activity, but they also provide a variety of creative movement alternatives in the event of a relapse.

Financial. The Adaptive Equipment Loan Program (AELP) is a financial assistance program based in Maine with the mission to provide a creative, consumer-directed approach to financing for assistive technology (Adams, 2003). AELP offers low-interest, long-term loans for assistive technology given to Maine citizens with disabilities and their families as well as businesses and non-profits for access improvements that comply with the Americans with Disabilities Act (ADA) (Adams, 2003). The loan is used for the enhancement of independence/well-being. It can be used for work, school, home life, community life, health care, recreation, and/or leisure. AELP's board members understand that recreation and leisure are essential to a person's life, and are laxer on purchase limitations than most programs. Perhaps the most exciting aspect of this program is its treatment of the disabled individual; by giving them purchasing power it shows trust. In return, individuals with MS become active workers, consumers, and taxpayers. The community becomes accessible once again and independence is gained. These individuals can keep their jobs thanks to the adjustment initiatives they chose to pursue and their creative problem-solving capabilities. Participation in this program displays and encourages a willingness by the individual to adapt to achieve the quality of life they desire.

Creative problem solving. Familiar creative problem-solving methods have been used in medical environments as a way to improve communication between health care providers and patients (Col, Solomon, Springmann, Garbin, Ionete, Pbert, Alvarez, Tierman, Hopson, Kutz, Morales, Griffin, Phillips, & Ngo, 2017). Value Clarification Exercises (VCE) help patients with MS determine what matters most on a personal level when making a health decision (Col et al., 2017). A card sorting tool, similar to the one utilized in the creative problem solving process, is used throughout these exercises to help patients organize their thoughts into a hierarchal map (Col et. al., 2017). Simplifying the language and allowing the patient's voice to be heard creates meaningful dialogue and improvements in disease management. This is a tremendous move towards progress of integrating creative thinking within the medical industry (Col et al., 2017).

Creative arts. The arts also have a profound effect on the lives of those living with MS. Creative arts programs have helped to establish creative thinking skills, promote creative expression, and create opportunities for esteem development (River et al., 2017). Studies have shown that creative arts participation leads to a sense of choice and control, empowerment, increased self-confidence, and a sense of personal achievement (Perruzza & Kinsella, 2010). Companies like Dick Blick Art Materials sell adaptive art tools for those in need of assistance while creating (Uhland, 2013). Local MS Society chapters offer a variety of classes and group activities focusing on creative arts (Uhland, 2013).

Survivor Arts Project, which began in 2006, is a traveling art exhibition which allows those with disabilities and mental health disorders to display their work (creating a sense of empowerment & achievement), encourage conversation, and to break down barriers (River et al., 2017). Recovery through Arts (RtA) programs are used as an avenue for exposure to more creative art forms/experiential exercises and people with disabilities and/or mental health disorders help to develop and run the workshops. The focus is on teaching communication, relationship building, developing personal insight and professional empathy through the language of creative arts (River et al., 2017). Arts All Over The Place, created in 2006 by the NHS Birmingham Social Inclusion Team, offers creative arts workshops and free exhibition space to showcase the work of people with disabilities. The goal is to challenge social stigma and celebrate well-being (River et al., 2017).

Technology. Technology has allowed for unparalleled global communication and creative collaboration. In relation to MS, it means both independence and community. Apps like PatientsLikeMe, HealthVault, ResearchKit, and SymTrac are health data-sharing platforms where the patient records and monitors their symptoms, perhaps discovering patterns which can help to manage the disease (Feys et al., 2016). The patient's feedback can lead to accelerated research, better treatments, and maybe even a cure. TRHLAB, developed by the Hospital de la Santa Creu I Sant Pau in Barcelona, offers speech therapy at home via videotaped exercises and feedback via Skype (Feys et al., 2016). Video platforms have helped to make creative learning more accessible than ever for those with progressive MS.

As technology advances, it is also helping create access for rural populations. The Women to Women project was an 11-week computer intervention program that provided health education and support to rural women with chronic illnesses, with the goal of discovering how they chose to adapt to their disease. To help them adapt to better living, the use of virtual support groups was implemented, which in turn behaved as a record for the study (Kelly et al., 2012). This not only provided information on an underrepresented population, but also gave these women the gift of a creative community.

The Unmet Creative Needs of Today

Patient partnerships. Patients are crucial to research. Including patients as active partners in research offers the potential to improve research design and logistics. Their input can help to contribute to the framework of trial design, developing/implementing strategies for participant recruitment, retention, and increasing the dissemination of the trial results (Smith, 2017). More research should also be conducted toward developing personal strategies for living a better life with MS (Salamonsen, Launsø, Kruse, & Eriksen, 2010). Most studies focus on the quality of life regarding symptom management, and not on strategic planning. The medical field should be tapping into the patient's point of view as an information source and establishing a creative partnership. Health care providers would be doing their patient's a favor by encouraging personal ownership and decision-making, while providing data that supports its benefits (Feys et al., 2016).

Neurological development. Regarding neural developments, exploration of neural flexibilities (cognitive processing strategies that enable adaptability to new and unexpected conditions) and exploitations (techniques that repair, replace, or enhance neural properties), as well as how they can be manipulated for symptom management, would be an area worth investing (Mechsner, 2004). Neuroscientists should continue to develop further research into the relationship of the corpus callosum and divergent thinking processes to determine any new findings (Moore, Bhadelia, Billings, Fulwiler, Heilman, Rood, & Gansler, 2009).

Creative programming. Creative arts should play an active part in MS patient's lives whether it is through programming, studies, therapy, or policy. Numerous studies, such as Survivor Arts Project, Women-to-Women, and Recovery Through Arts, support the use of creative arts as a coping mechanism, a tool for expression, or career opportunity, so it would follow that it would be a major priority for application. It is worth campaigning for creative arts access in healthcare environments due to its value in recovery and mental well-being (Kelly et al., 2012, River et al., 2017).

Creative arts need to be made available beyond the urban/suburban boundaries and into rural populations (Kelly et al., 2012). The geographical divide can be overcome through technology, program development, and healthcare awareness. Art as a complementary therapy should also be further explored as a nonpharmacological alternative to traditional pain management (Kelly et al., 2012).

Social stigmas in the workforce. Inaccuracies in the portrayal of individuals with MS will conclude my analysis of unmet creative needs within the MS community. It is time for society to reframe their perceptions of people with disabilities. These misconceptions lead to high unemployment rates, financial distress, and feelings of social exile, all of which restrict creative growth.

As someone who has experienced such discrimination I believe I must call attention to this issue. Within businesses, patients can facilitate management learning meetings to achieve an empathetic environment. Organize meetings where management and coworkers can learn more about MS and initiate constructive discussion to prevent less than ideal assumptions and beliefs (Vickers, 2011). As a manager or coworker, show compassion and understand that they are no different than you. Give them room to explore methods of adjustment. Allow them to demonstrate their problem-solving skills. If they were valuable employees before their diagnosis, chances are they are just as valuable now.

Social stigmas in financial institutions. The stigmas within financial institutions are much like those in the workforce. By treating disabled people as financially irresponsible (Adams, 2003), they prevent assistive technology from reaching the hands of someone who is trying their best to adapt to their new world. Assistive technology has a collateral value which can be used to secure a loan. It also makes the individual more employable which increases their income and loan repayment rate (Adams, 2003). People with MS do not strive to become the burdens of society; they are treated that way until they become a product of their environment. Given the appropriate resources, they are more than capable of figuring the rest out.

Personal accountability. For those who have been diagnosed with MS there comes a certain responsibility and accountability in one's approach to this new life. It is not easy, and it never will be, but with the right mindset, life can improve. Adjusting one's attitude towards the disease and creating a positive approach will increase motivation to work with the disease and not against it (Olenik, 2006). Reworking one's language can improve one's outlook and encourage change. Viewing a wheelchair as a means of achieving greater mobility as opposed to a symbol of invalidism is an example of language adjustment (Nichols, 1971).

Regardless of opinion or feeling, MS is a learning process in and of itself, and will continue to be until there is a cure. This disease requires constant problem-solving to cooperate with changing deficiencies and with a malfunctioning central nervous system, learning creativity can be a challenge. While it will take an extraordinary amount of perseverance to reach a baseline, I believe it can be done.

Final Thoughts

The day I was diagnosed I called off work and sat in a coffee shop for hours. I cannot remember whether I cried, laughed, or did both at the same time, but I do remember promising myself to live purposefully. That was more or less my mantra growing up, but life has a way of softening the edges by creating an agenda called "tomorrow." My diagnosis triggered the need to center myself and focus on a current state of existence.

Margaret Vickers (2015) recounts her MS diagnosis,

> But the really good thing about *my heartbreak* has been that it has helped me recognize and zero in on the heartbreak of others—especially those with MS—even when their heartbreak is held in the chains of their too few words. (p. 85)

Multiple sclerosis does impact the ability to learn creativity, but not in the way I had anticipated. Under a conditional basis, the brain can disparage idea generation creating a neural limitation to the learning process (Mechsner, 2004). However, the real source of impact stems from society's treatment of people with MS impacting creativity engagement.

What led me to this big question was the recognition that I see potential, where others see loss. I want others with MS to know that we can learn to live fully through creativity. Yes, there are neural discrepancies that may prevent us from being great ideators, but we can still be damn good implementors!

References

Adams, K. (2003). Maine's adaptive equipment loan program: Creative financing for assistive technology. *Journal of Disability Policy Studies, 14(2)*, 82-85.

Boje, D. (2001). *Narrative methods for organizational and communication research*. London, UK: Sage Publications.

Brown, W., Paul, L.K., Symington, M., & Dietrich, R. (2005). Comprehension of humor in primary agenesis of the corpus callosum. *Neuropsychologia, 43*, 906-916.

Chen, R.K., Glover-Graf, N.M., & Marini, I. (2011). Religion and spirituality in the lives of people with multiple sclerosis. *Journal of Religion, Disability & Health, 15(3)*, 254-271.

Col, N., Solomon, A.J., Springmann, V., Garbin, C.P., Ionete, C., Pbert, L., et al. (2017). Whose preferences matter? A patient-centered approach for eliciting treatment goals. *Medical Decision Making*, DOI: 10.1177/0272989X17724434.

Compston, A., & Coles, A. (2002). Multiple sclerosis. *The Lancet, 359*, 1221-1231.

Csikszentmihalyi, M. (1990). *Flow: The psychology of optimal experience.* New York, NY: Harper Collins.

Dobkin, B. (2009). Collaborative models for translational neuroscience and rehabilitation research. *Neurorehabilitation and Neural Repair, 23(7)*, 633-640.

Doward, L.C., McKenna, S.P., Meads, D.M., Twiss, J., & Eckert, B.J. (2009). The development of patient-reported outcome indices for multiple sclerosis. *Multiple Sclerosis, 15*, 1092-1102.

Dutton, J.E., Worline, M.C., Frost, P.J., & Lilius, J. (2006). Explaining compassion organizing. *Administrative Science Quarterly, 51(1)*, 59-96.

Falvo, D. (2009). *Medical and psychosocial aspects of chronic illness and disability.* Sudbury, MA: Jones & Barlett.

Feys, P., Giovannoni, G., Dijsselbloem, N., Centonze, D., Eelen, P., & Andersen, S.L. (2016). The importance of a multi-disciplinary perspective and patient activation programmes in MS management. *Multiple Sclerosis Journal, 22(2S)*, 34-46.

Gray, D. (2007). Facilitating management learning: Developing critical reflection through reflective tools. *Management Learning, 38(5)*, 495-517.

Hamer, M. (2006). *The barefoot helper: Mindfulness and creativity in social work and the helping professions.* Lyme Regis, UK: Russell House Publishing.

Heilman, K. (2005). *Creativity and the brain.* New York, NY: Psychology Press.

Hunt, L., Nikopoulou-Smyrni, P., & Reynolds, F. (2014). "It gave me something big in my life to wonder and think about which took over the space...and not MS": Managing well-being in multiple sclerosis through art-making. *Disability & Rehabilitation, 36(4)*, 1139-1147.

Kelly, C., Cudney, S., & Weinert, C. (2012). Use of creative arts as a complementary therapy by rural women coping with chronic illness. *Journal of Holistic Nursing, 30(1)*, 48-54.

Koch, L.C., Rumrill, P.D., Roessler, R.T., & Fitzgerald, S.M. (2001). Illness and demographic correlates of quality of life among people with multiple sclerosis. *Rehabilitation Psychology, 46(2)*, 154-164.

Kraft, G.H., Freal, J.E., & Coryell, J.K. (1986). Disability, disease duration, and rehabilitation service needs in multiple sclerosis: Patient perspectives. *Archives of Physical and Medical Rehabilitation, 67(3)*, 164-168.

Lewis, R. (1979). Organic signs, creativity, and personality characteristics of patients following cerebral commissurotomy. *Clinical Neuropsychology, 1*, 29-33.

Lohne, V., Aasgaard, T., Caspari, S., Slettebo, A., & Naden, D. (2010). The lonely battle for dignity: Individuals struggling with multiple sclerosis. *Nursing Ethics, 17(3)*, 301-311.

Marrie, R.A., Cutter, G., & Tyry, T. (2011). Substantial adverse association of visual and vascular comorbidities on visual disability in multiple sclerosis. *Multiple Sclerosis Journal, 17(12)*, 1464-1471.

Mechsner, F. (2004). A psychological approach to human voluntary movements. *Journal of Motor Behavior, 36(4)*, 355-370.

Moore, D., Bhadelia, R., Billings, R., Fulwiler, C., Heilman, K., Rood, K., et al. (2009). Hemispheric connectivity and the visual-spatial divergent-thinking component of creativity. *Brain and Cognition, 70*, 267-272.

Nichols, P. (1971). Some problems in rehabilitation of the severely disabled. *Proceedings of the Royal Society of Medicine, 64*, 349-353.

Olenik, L. (2006). Responding to multiple sclerosis: The PACE model part 3: Movement and the stress response. *Palaestra, 22(3)*, 20-25.

Paul, L.K., Schieffer, B., & Brown, W.S. (2004). Social processing deficits in primary agenesis of the corpus callosum: Narratives from the Thematic Apperception Test. *Archives of Clinical Neuropsychology, 19*, 215-225.

Perruzza, N., & Kinsella, E.A. (2010). Creative arts occupations in therapeutic practice: A review of the literature. *British Journal of Occupational Therapy, 73(6)*, 261-268.

Powers, S.K., Dodd, S.L., & Noland, V.J. (2005). *Total fitness and wellness*. San Francisco, CA: Pearson Benjamin Cummings.

Reynolds, F. (2004). Conversations about creativity and chronic illness II: Textile artists coping with long-term health problems reflect on the creative process. *Creativity Research Journal, 16 1)*, 79-89.

River, D.H.M., Thakoordin, J.M., & Billing, L. (2017). Creativity in social work education and practice: Reflections on a Survivor Arts Project. *Social Work Education, 36(7)*, 758-774.

Rodriguez de Romo, A. (2007). Chance, creativity, and the discovery of the nerve growth factor. *Journal of the History of the Neurosciences, 16(3)*, 268-287.

Salamonsen, A., Launso, L., Kruse, T.E., & Eriksen, S.H. (2010). Understanding unexpected courses of multiple sclerosis among patients using complementary and alternative medicine: A travel from recipient to explorer. *International Journal of Qualitative Studies on Health and Well-being, 5(2)*, DOI: 10.3402/qhw.v5i2.5032.

Schmid, T. (2005). *Promoting health through creativity for professionals in healthcare arts and education.* London, UK: Whurr.

Smith, K. (2017). The evolving role of people with MS in clinical research—Some progress but more is needed. *Multiple Sclerosis Journal, 23(12)*, 1579-1582.

Thompson, M., & Blair, S.E. (1998). Creative arts in occupational therapy: Ancient history or contemporary practice? *Occupational Therapy International, 5(5)*, 48-64.

Uhland, V. (2013). The picture of health. *Momentum, 6(3)*, 42-45.

Vickers, M. (2010). The creation of fiction to share other truths and different viewpoints: A creative journey and an interpretive process. *Qualitative Inquiry, 16(7)*, 556-565.

Vickers, M. (2011). Taking a compassionate turn for workers with multiple sclerosis (MS): Towards the facilitation of management learning. *Management Learning, 42(1)*, 49-65.

Vickers, M. (2015). Stories, disability, and "dirty" workers: Creative writing to go beyond too few words. *Journal of Management Inquiry, 24(1)*, 82-89.

Vrkljan, B., & Miller-Polgar, J. (2001). Meaning of occupational engagement in life-threatening illness: A qualitative pilot project. *Canadian Journal of Occupational Therapy, 68(4)*, 237-246.

About the Author

Danielle Myers is based in the countryside of Western New York where she researches, designs, and develops creativity initiatives through visual art programs. She holds a Master's degree in Creative Studies and a Bachelor's degree in Art at SUNY Buffalo State.

Danielle is a teaching artist and small business owner with a certificate in Entrepreneurship in the Arts from the Small Business Development Center at Buffalo State. Her involvement with the Western New York Book Art Center has led her to lead workshops in papermaking, printmaking, and bookbinding. This partnership led to Master Teaching Artists work for the Young Audiences of Western New York apprentice-program, ArtWorks, where she specialized in teaching book arts and professionalism to a group of young apprentices over a six-week period throughout the summer.

Danielle is a 2017 recipient of the Sidney J. Parnes & Ruth B. Noller Creativity Award from the International Center for Studies in Creativity at Buffalo State.

Email: danielle@dmyerscreativity.com
Website: www.dmyerscreativity.com

Can Creativity Help Children in Foster Care Transition From Surviving to Thriving?

Emilie Kenneally
International Center for Studies in Creativity
SUNY Buffalo State

Abstract

Children in foster care exhibit innate creative strengths and resilience that help them survive trauma and adverse situations. These children go through Adverse Childhood Experiences (ACEs; Gunderson Health System, 2014) that can impede their neurodevelopment and thinking skills, including those skills related to creativity and problem-solving. This paper explores the idea that bringing creativity skills to children in foster care can help them thrive, rather than just survive, and can improve their resilience and overall well-being.

Can Creativity Help Children in Foster Care Transition From Surviving to Thriving?

Imagine you are driving home from work in the early evening on a busy street. While stopped at a red light, you notice something coming toward your car from the opposite direction. It is difficult to see what the object is, but it appears to be smaller than a car. When the object gets closer, you can see that it is two toddlers driving a battery operated car down the middle of the street. The children have shaved heads and are dirty and disheveled. A passerby stops the children and asks them where their mother is, but the children only speak Spanish. The passerby takes out a cell phone to call the police. The next day, you wonder what happened to them. What you do not know is that the children were left home alone with their five-year-old brother while their father was at work and their mother went to look for drugs. The children were hungry and left the house to find food. The children are girls, twins in fact, though authorities initially thought they were boys because of their shaved heads. Police will find the twins' brother the following day, and all three children will enter the foster care system.

Stories like this one are heartbreaking and emotional. While it is sad that some children have experiences like this, there are positive aspects to the story. This anecdote illustrates the innate creative strengths that children in neglectful or abusive situations have that help them survive and develop resilience. Many of these children end up in foster care due to issues that are present in their biological families.

As someone who works in foster care, I have seen firsthand how children have used creativity to overcome trauma and neglect. This paper will explore how creativity might help children in foster care turn their survival skills into lasting life skills that could help them find long term success.

Foster Care

Many people do not have an accurate picture of the foster care system and what life is like for children in care. Foster care is seen as a solution for children whose parents are unwilling, unfit, or unable to care for them. Children are placed in foster care for a variety of reasons including abandonment, poverty, neglect, physical and sexual abuse, parental drug use, and parental psychopathology (Ferrera et al., 2013). According to the Department of Health and Human Services, there are 500,000 children served annually by the United States' foster care system, with 300,000 children exiting and entering the system each year (Connell, Katz, Saunders, & Tebes, 2006). This means that there is a large population of children each year that are displaced from their homes after experiencing traumatic situations.

Nearly half of the children that are in foster care stay in care for over one year, with the average length of stay being two years (Pecora et al., 2006). However, there are also children that spend most of their childhood living in the system. On average, approximately 21,000 children are emancipated from foster care each year because they have reached adulthood. Many of these children are ill-prepared to live independently after they are discharged from foster care. These youths are at a higher risk for victimization, poverty, dropping out of high school, homelessness, unemployment, and job instability (Affronti, Rittner, & Semanchin, 2015).

The goal for every child that enters foster care is permanency, meaning they obtain a safe, long-term living situation. This can be achieved through the child returning home to their biological family, adoption, living with a relative, or taking part in an independent living program.

Reunification with a child's biological family is highly likely after they initially enter care. This decreases in likelihood around the tenth month of the child being in care; The greatest chance of adoption occurs between nine to eighteen months of being in foster care (Connell et al., 2006). Some children also run away from their foster care placement, which is referred to as being AWOL (absent without leave). Children in foster care are at a higher risk for mental health issues due to the traumas they have experienced (Ferrera et al., 2013), and on average they show higher levels of externalizing and internalizing behaviors than children that received appropriate care from their parents (Lawrence, Carlson, & Egeland, 2006). Often, foster parents are not fully equipped to handle these behaviors, which can lead to the disruption of the child's placement.

Disruption, or the sudden ending of a current placement and subsequent move to a new placement, can have negative effects on a child's mental and emotional stability. Other risk factors can lead to the disruption of a placement, such as age (older children are more likely to disrupt), gender (girls are more likely to disrupt), and having a background of many residential placements (Oosterman, Schuengel, Slot, Bullens, & Doreleijers 2006).

The negative consequences of being in foster care can follow a child through adolescence and into adulthood. Children that have been in foster care are more likely to have mental health issues as an adult, are more likely to be arrested, are less likely to be able to develop appropriate relationships with caregivers and peers, and they may struggle with emotional dysregulation (Leve et al., 2012).

In a study conducted to understand the lasting effects foster care had on children, individuals who had been in care as teens were interviewed to see what their lives were like as adults (Pecora et al., 2006). Less than a third of the participants reported having resources to support themselves upon leaving foster care. Two in five participants attended college, and only 2.7 % earned a bachelor's degree (as compared to the national average of 24.4%) (Pecora et al., 2006). One in five participants had experienced homelessness and many lived in households at or below the poverty line (Pecora et al., 2006). These results show that without a viable permanency option and intense services, many children that were in foster care slip through the cracks and develop issues that follow them into adulthood.

Resilience

While children in foster care are more vulnerable than those who have never been placed in care, they may also develop a stronger resilience to cope with the trauma of their past. Children that are resilient have social competence (such as empathy and communication skills), problem-solving skills, critical consciousness (insightful awareness), autonomy, and a sense of purpose (Davidson-Arad & Navaro-Bitton, 2015). These children can survive and succeed under sustained stress and hardship and are able to overcome negative environmental factors and experiences. These adaptations help to minimize the negative impact of risk factors on development (Davidson-Arad & Navaro-Bitton, 2015). When a child is resilient, he or she can be as successful as a child who lived in a nurturing family setting.

How does resilience develop? When a child experiences home, peer, school, and community environments that are rich in external assets, they develop internal assets that are associated with healthy development and learning (Davidson-Arad & Navaro-Bitton, 2015). External assets are things like caring relationships, high expectations, and meaningful participation in a family, while internal assets include cooperation, communication, self-efficacy, empathy, problem-solving skills, self-awareness, goals, and aspirations (Davidson-Arad & Navaro-Bitton, 2015). In essence, children need the help of adults and those around them to develop these internal skills, which helps them to be more resilient.

Resilience can develop in more than just supportive environments. Many of the children in foster care have developed resilience as a response to the negative home environments in which they were living. The children that left home in their battery-operated car are a prime example: they experienced a negative situation (an absent parent and being hungry) and came up with a way to overcome these issues.

This type of resilience is often used by foster children to meet their own needs for safety, clothing, shelter, food, and love. In many cases, these children are so focused on survival that they do not have the opportunity to thrive and be successful – they are just trying to "get by." Since these children are already showing resilience and creativity in how they overcome challenges, it appears that creativity skills could help children in foster care move past survival and thrive in their placements and their lives.

Adverse Childhood Experiences and Thinking Skills

The Adverse Childhood Experience (ACE) Study (Gunderson Health System, 2014) explored the lasting effect that traumatic experiences have on children later in life and confirmed that adversity early in life could lead to physical, mental, and emotional issues in adulthood. Gunderson Health System (2014) showed how infants' brains are a clean slate that are waiting to learn from experiences. At this stage, an infant's brain only has the neural connections that it needs (such as connections that help the infant cry when hungry). Once a child reaches elementary school, most of the brain's wiring has been established based on the experiences that the child has had thus far, a process known as arborization (Gunderson Health System, 2014). Experiences that occur most often form stronger neural connections. When the child reaches puberty, a process called pruning takes place, and the least experienced connections in the brain begin to fade (Gunderson Health System, 2014).

Traumatic events can impede the developmental processes that occur in the brain: when a child experiences stress or trauma, the limbic system is negatively affected (Gunderson Health System, 2014). This system regulates hormones, mood, and affects learning and memory. The hippocampus and amygdala are part of this system and regulate panic, fear, and impulse (the fight or flight response). When children experience ACEs, they are constantly in a state of fear and uncertainty, which causes negative situations and responses to be strongly wired in the child's brain (Gunderson Health System, 2014). Living a life in turmoil can force a child to develop negative coping mechanisms (such as using drugs or self-harming) and embed those responses in the brain (Gunderson Health System, 2014). When the brain is constantly focused on responding to stressors, a child is not learning basic thinking skills or healthy stress responses. Children who have dealt with ACEs often also struggle with emotional regulation (Gunderson Health System, 2014).

Basic thinking skills, such as those used in creativity, are a key part of an individual's potential. Thinking skills can help an individual adapt to challenges, prompt innovation, and lead to personal fulfillment (Antonietti, 2009), and early childhood is the most fruitful time for an individual to acquire these skills. Antonietti (2009) introduced four different ways of learning that contribute to a child's thinking skills. The first is learning through exploration: children should be given the opportunity to explore their environments and observe patterns in personal interactions. The second is learning through direct instruction: children should be taught strategies that can help them solve problems, make decisions, and create something new. The third is learning through transfer to real life: children should be guided to see corresponding ideas between the instructional setting and real-life situations. And the fourth way of learning is through attitude change: children should learn to overcome the negative aspects of a situation by adopting productive and innovative perspectives (Antonietti, 2009).

But many children in foster care miss the opportunity to fully develop their basic thinking skills, as they tend to apply their focus to surviving ACEs. These children do not have the opportunity to learn in Antonietti's (2009) ways for any number of reasons. These children's biological parents may have been dealing with issues of their own and may not have been able to teach these thinking skills, or might lack these skills themselves, and are therefore unable to pass them on to their children.

Because these children are in survival mode, they are often using creativity skills just to make it to the next day, rather than to thrive and be successful. Antonietti (2009) stated that thinking skills could help a child self-reflect, which can help them develop self-regulation. Self-regulation can help a child problem solve and better respond to stressors. Once children are living in a permanent situation or the issues that brought them into foster care are resolved, they can refocus their attention on enhancing their thinking skills. This will help them more fully access their creativity and use it to be successful adults who are engaged in society, rather than using creativity just to survive.

Creativity and Well-Being

Creativity can also support a person's overall health and well-being (Gordon & O'Toole, 2015). There are key competences—complex constructs that are composed of different elements of knowledge, skills, and attitudes—needed for effective human action in any particular domain (Gordon & O'Toole, 2015). When teaching children, Gordon and O'Toole (2015) stressed the importance of focusing on creativity as a core competence.

Creativity can be expressed mentally, emotionally, and physically and can help children with self-regulation and problem-solving (Gordon & O'Toole 2015). Creativity is a systemic state involving the whole person, as is well-being. Well-being and creativity can both be nurtured through understanding the diverse ways in which children learn, communicate, and develop. Once a child understands the way that he or she processes and learns, that child can then function in a more creative, innovative, and generative way. When the adults in a child's life understand these inner differences, they can then encourage the unfolding of each child's unique potential and an understanding of the child's inner processes, ultimately encouraging the child to be more creative (Gordon & O'Toole 2015).

There are multiple ways to help a child learn for well-being, and therefore creativity. Adults should create a receptive environment for children and model openness to differences. Adults should allow children to share their learning processes by giving them choices and time for self-reflection. There should be an emphasis on self-discovery and a holistic approach to the child's learning. In learning different cognitive skills, like creativity, children will be more likely to lead happy, healthy lives in which they feel recognized and accepted for who they are. Achieving a state of well-being can also help a child live and function in society through personal fulfillment and development, active citizenship, social inclusion, and employment (Gordon & O'Toole, 2015).

Conclusion

If you were able to follow the children that had been riding down the street in their toy car, you would see that they are now two beautiful, happy twin girls. They are thriving in a foster home, and are using their creativity skills to do things like take dance classes and enhance their bilingualism. In other words, their creativity skills are being used to help them thrive and develop on a daily basis, rather than simply to survive. They are a perfect example of how children can overcome adverse situations and develop new cognitive skills. While these girls clearly had innate creativity and problem-solving skills, these skills are now being further enhanced and used in a much wider variety of ways than to find food. These girls stand a better chance of being successful adults and leading fulfilling lives, and are living proof that creativity can contribute to a child's well-being and overall cognitive strength and can help them thrive rather than just "get by" in life, even if they faced adversity at a young age.

Further research on this topic could be ground-breaking. Researchers could delve into the possibilities opened up by linking creativity to well-being, especially when looking through the lens of foster care. Can these creativity skills lead to better outcomes for foster children over their lifetimes? Researching this topic in depth would be worthwhile. Another important step could be helping foster parents to recognize children's creative strengths, and how to use those strengths to help them adjust to their placements and thrive. Stories like the twins' could become the foundation for showing that children's innate creativity can be nourished to help them succeed.

References

Affronti, M., Rittner, B., & Semanchin Jones, A. M. (2015). Functional adaptation to foster care: Foster care alumni speak out. *Journal of Public Child Welfare, 9*, 1-21.

Antonietti, A. (2009). Investing in the human potential: Improving cognitive life skills in young people. *Rivista Internazionale di Scienze Sociali, 117*, 477-492.

Connell, C. M., Katz, K. H., Saunders, L., & Tebes, J. K. (2006). Leaving foster care: The influence of child and case characteristics on foster care exit rates. *Children and Youth Services Review, 28*, 780-798.

Davidson-Arad, B., & Navaro-Bitton, I. (2015). Resilience among adolescents in foster care. *Children and Youth Services Review, 59*, 63-70.

Ferrara, P., Romani, L., Bottaro, G., Ianniello, F., Fabrizio, G. C., Chiaretti, A., & Alvaro, F. (2013). The physical and mental health of children in foster care. *Iranian Journal of Public Health, 42*, 368-373.

Gordon, J., & O'Toole, L. (2015). Learning for well-being: Creativity and inner diversity. *Cambridge Journal of Education, 45*, 333-346.

Gunderson Health System. (2014). Adverse childhood experiences (ACE) study: Identify, intervene, and interrupt [Online training video]. Retrieved from http://mediasite.gundluth.org/Mediasite/Play/6c9c48e551a840d586392974eca729271d

Lawrence, C. R., Carlson, E. A., & Egeland, B. (2006). The impact of foster care on development. *Development and Psychopathology, 18*, 57-76.

Leve, L. D., Harold, G. T., Chamberlain, P., Landsverk, J. A., Fisher, P. A., & Vostanis, P. (2012). Practitioner review: Children in foster care – Vulnerabilities and evidence-based interventions that promote resilience processes. *The Journal of Child Psychology and Psychiatry, 53*, 1197-1211.

Oosterman, M., Schuengel, C., Slot, N. W., Bullens, R. A. R., & Doreleijers, T. A. H. (2006). Disruptions in foster care: A review and meta-analysis. *Children and Youth Services Review, 29,* 53-76.

Pecora, P. J., Kessler, R. C., O'Brien, K., White, C. R., Williams, J., Hiripi, E., ...Herrick, M. A. (2006). Educational and employment outcomes of adults formerly placed in foster care: Results from the Northwest Foster Care Alumni Study. *Children and Youth Services Review, 28,* 1459-1481.

About the Author

Emilie Kenneally graduated with her Bachelor's Degree in Social Work from SUNY Buffalo State and recently completed her Master's in Creativity and Change Leadership at the International Center for Studies in Creativity at Buffalo State. While pursuing her Master's, Emilie was the recipient of the Sidney J. Parnes and Ruth B. Noller Creativity Award. Emilie currently works as a foster care case worker at a nonprofit agency. Her interests lie in using creativity for social innovation and to change the way that social services are delivered to clients.

Email: emiazga27@yahoo.com

Are Individuals in Poverty More Creative?

Cher Ravenell
International Center for Studies in Creativity
SUNY Buffalo State

Abstract

Research suggests that those who have fewer resources may be more creative with less. Whether scarcity has a positive or negative impact on creativity depends on the individual's mindset. Those who are in poverty must address urgent concerns related to survival. This constant state of urgency leaves limited time for long-term planning and growth. Therefore, those in poverty are unable to gain leverage to pull themselves out of poverty. Limitations, external and self-imposed, appear to be at the core of the problem. Self-imposed barriers and habits play a large part in determining whether creativity is expressed. Issues such as extreme stress and health problems may cause a reduction in energy levels—which is a key component in creativity. External influences such as social policy, limited education choices, and the immediate environment could cause creativity to be reduced. More often than not, government policies limit economic mobility.

Are Individuals in Poverty More Creative?

As a child, one of my favorite things was to stay overnight with my grandparents. My childhood is filled with memories of taking the bus downtown with my Nana, sitting in the kitchen as she made homemade bread, helping her hang laundry, and going to the grocery store with her. It wasn't until I was much older that I began to think, *Why does she make homemade bread instead of buying it? Why doesn't she throw her clothes in the dryer instead of hanging them on a line? Why does she walk to the store and buy a minimal amount of food that gets cooked that night? Why doesn't she call a cab or drive a car?* It wasn't until I was much older that I realized that my grandparents were poor.

As with many of my contemporaries, I never knew what it was like to live in poverty. I grew up in suburbia. My biggest choices involved *what* or *where* I was going to eat, *what* I was going to wear, or *where* was I going to go after school. It was not *how* I was going to get food to eat, *how* I was going to get clothes to wear, *how* I would get to school, nor *how* my peers would treat me while I was there. In poverty, choices regarding what is workable are different, problems can appear larger, thinking falls into old habits, and options can seem limited. Does the separation of *what* vs. *how* mean those who live in poverty are more creative because they have to answer *how* regularly?

Poverty in the United States

To qualify as living in poverty in the United States, I looked at two factors: what constitutes poverty and who qualifies as impoverished. According to the U.S. Census Bureau (2017):

> The official poverty definition uses money income before taxes and does not include capital gains or noncash benefits (such as public housing, Medicaid, and food stamps). The Census Bureau uses a set of money income thresholds that vary by family size and composition to determine who is in poverty. If a family's total income is less than the family's threshold, then that family and every individual in it is considered in poverty. The official poverty thresholds do not vary geographically, but they are updated for inflation using the Consumer Price Index (CPI-U).

The thresholds are intended for use as a statistical yardstick, not as a complete description of what people and families need to live. Based on reported income, 33% of the United States population—or 105 million people—live close to poverty, with incomes less than two times that of their poverty thresholds (Benson, 2017).

While the official 2016 poverty rate was 12.7% and an estimated 43.1 million Americans lived in poverty (Samega, Fontenot, & Kollar, 2017), there are reported issues with these numbers. The major issue is that poverty estimates do not include people who are homeless, college students, institutionalized, or noncitizens. The rate also excludes military personnel who do not live with at least one civilian adult (U.S. Census Bureau, 2017). Based on the data collected, one-third of the population of the United States, or over 100 million individuals live below, at, or just above the poverty level. To say that a third of the population is more creative than the other two thirds solely based on economic status is unreasonable, so I concentrated on those individuals who live in what is called *deep* and *extreme poverty*.

Deep poverty is defined as living in a household with a total cash income below 50% of the poverty threshold. Those in deep poverty represented 6.1% of the total population and 45% of those in poverty. Deep poverty tends to be a chronic condition that persists generation after generation. Half of those in deep poverty are under 25 years of age, and more than one third are single mothers and their children. Three percent of children live at least half of their childhood in deep poverty. Using the criteria set by the World Bank, deep poverty means living on $2 per day per person or less. (UC Davis Center for Poverty Research, 2017). The number of U.S. households living on $2 per day per person or less is 1.46 million. This is a total of $14 per week for each person in the household. But are these individuals more creative than 94% of the U.S. population?

Based on the above definition, my grandparents lived in poverty, perhaps even deep poverty. They had one income, six children, lived in public housing, and often sustained themselves on public surplus food. It was not uncommon to see my grandmother organizing the monthly bills using the "envelope system" of budgeting for the groceries (Cruze, 2017). She was very resourceful regarding how and where money was spent. She spent what she had and nothing more. Anything leftover was saved for emergencies. She spent much of her time organizing how their resources would be allocated and how she could get as much as she could for as little money as possible.

How is Creativity Presented in Deep Poverty?

The question here is not whether those in deep poverty are creative, but *how* are they creative? In what ways do they present ideas? How do they experience and interpret those ideas?

> It has been shown that those who experience resource scarcity, similar to those who live in deep poverty, have a constraint mindset that manifests itself through increased novelty in product use. These limits force consumers to think beyond the traditional functionality of a given product. This enhances product-use creativity. (Mehta & Zhu, 2016)

Based on this finding, it is suggested that those who have little do more with what they already have. I recall a story from a colleague that she did not know how to make coffee in a coffeemaker until she came to college. As she was growing up, coffee was boiled in a pot, and a sock was used to strain the grounds into a cup. Due to lack of money to buy a coffeemaker, her family did what they could with what they had. This example reinforces the point made by Mehta & Zhu: The impoverished find more uses for everyday products. Further research suggests that scarcity might facilitate creativity for those in deep poverty (Hill, 2001).

Scarcity is shown to spark more creativity and increase creative behaviors. Scarcity prioritizes our choices and it can make us more effective. Scarcity creates a powerful goal dealing with pressing needs and ignoring other goals (Heshmat, 2015). Research in creative cognition has shown that individuals are more creative when limited by constraints (University of Illinois at Urbana-Champaign, 2015). By default, does this mean that those who experience deep poverty or those who have less are on average more creative? For example, the following items have been inducted into the National Toy Hall of Fame at the Strong National Museum of Play: a box, a stick, a blanket, and a ball (Grebey, 2017). When we look at scarcity in relation to excess: If all you had was a stick to play with (scarcity), you would probably come up with many ideas of how to use the stick as a toy. If you have an excess of toys as well as the stick, you may never play with it, therefore decreasing your divergence in regards to the ideas of how you use the stick.

Financial constraints have been shown to not be an obstacle to creativity but rather an igniter of creativity (Scopelliti, Cillo, Busacca, & Mazursky, 2014). While both scarcities of product and money have been proven to increase creativity, how is it that those in deep poverty rarely seem to make strides in their economic growth? Let's consider the work of Maslow (1943) and his *hierarchy of needs*. These include, in order of importance: basic needs, safety, belonging and love, esteem, and self-actualization. Maslow argued that the current and most pressing needs motivate individuals:

> These basic goals are related to each other, being arranged in a hierarchy of prepotency. This means that the most prepotent goal will monopolize consciousness and will tend of itself to organize the recruitment of the various capacities of the organism. The less prepotent needs are [p. 395] minimized, even forgotten or denied. But when a need is fairly well satisfied, the next prepotent ('higher') need emerges, in turn to dominate the conscious life and to serve as the center of organization of behavior, since gratified needs are not active motivators. (p. 394-395)

In deep poverty, individuals may not be able to fulfill the most basic of needs, which include hunger, shelter, and warmth. A person cannot move toward fulfilling other needs until they have met the previous need. Another answer could be that extreme financial constraints cause anxiety that could interfere with retrieval processes or memory recall; this, in turn, could inhibit ideation (Smith, Michael, & Hocevar, 2009).

One of the strongest indicators of creative thinking is a person's ability to ideate by engaging in divergent thinking (Runco, 2010). According to Runco (2004):

> Creativity is a syndrome or complex, and flexibility is an important part of it. A person's flexibility gives them the capacity to cope with the advances, opportunities, technologies, and changes that happen in his/her life. This implies that creativity is reactive and your creativity response reacts to problems or challenges. (p. 658)

If creativity is reactive, and those in deep poverty have shown themselves to be more adaptive and flexible in their daily lives due to their circumstances, could this mean that they react more creatively to challenges they face on a daily basis?

When engaged in formal creative problem solving, ideas are generated before the stakeholder converges. Even with an open mind, selecting ideas that have potential consumes time and energy. The stakeholder is guided to be deliberate and make choices based on the combination of novelty and usefulness. In deep poverty, additional factors need to be factored into those choices. While the divergent process may be the same across economic variables, factors such as the ability to meet basic needs reduces the number of viable options for those living in deep poverty because novelty requires a certain amount of risk-taking. Risk-taking is not a viable path when trying to meet one's basic needs for survival. Additional factors that impact choosing novel ideas may include lack of finances and time, poor health, and the inability to develop a workable plan. A lack of income could be considered a deal-breaker for some ideas. Ideas become more limited when the amount of viable solutions to pick from becomes less and less due to deal-breakers. With these limited options, choices have to be made as to what will work best even though it may not be the best solution to the problem. Often the choice is either to give up or be more creative by exploring avenues that stretch limitations and boundaries.

If people in deep poverty have the potential to be more creative, then why is this not recognized? Is it creativity at its most base level that goes unnoticed because of its lack of value to the general population? This could be explained by Beghetto and Kaufman's (2007) *little-c creativity. Little-c* is shown as intrapersonal creativity that is part of the learning process by people that have virtually no experience. The argument for *little-c* in deep poverty has not been studied, but fits in the framework of broader conceptions of creativity. The study of *little-c* as it relates to deep poverty may open new understanding of how people discover and apply new insights as well as when and where their creativity turns into little-c (Beghetto & Kaufman, 2007). There is potential that the high creativity level of those in deep poverty has been overlooked because it is creativity in everyday life. These instances may have very little value to a larger population but there are creative uses for every day products that are ignored due to more prominent innovations. Those in poverty are innovative but only through personal use of products on hand.

Creativity Deterrents in Deep Poverty

According to Evans (1993), barriers to creativity fall into two groups: *habits* and *blocks*. *Habits* help us to perform many of our daily activities, both personal and professional. Life conditions us to develop habits, and they become ingrained.

> Past behavior guides future responses through two processes. Well-practiced behaviors in constant contexts recur because the processing that initiates and controls their performance becomes automatic. Frequency of past behavior then reflects habit strength and has a direct effect on future performance. Alternately, when behaviors are not well learned or when they are performed in unstable or difficult contexts, conscious decision making is likely to be necessary to initiate and carry out the behavior. Under these conditions, past behavior (along with attitudes and subjective norms) may contribute to intentions, and behavior is guided by intentions. (Ouellette & Wood, 1998, p. 54)

However, habits can confine us to viewing the world in a conventional way. When habits hinder creativity, we fall into a rut (Evans, 1993). Habits are an example of *mental set fixation*, which means individuals do not explore out of their comfort zone when thinking of solutions. This has much to do with a person's past experiences. When you form habits that become ingrained, it is difficult to look at things from multiple viewpoints (Gilliard, n.d.). A person in poverty may stick to one way of doing something because they know it works and they are reluctant to take risks. Poverty taxes cognitive resources. It also means making painful trade-offs and sacrifices (Heshmat, 2015). In deep poverty, risk means expending resources and energy.

The other form of barrier to creativity is *blocks*. *Blocks* can be categorized as perpetual, emotional, cultural, environmental, intellectual and expressive. Perpetual blocks involve using what works. Emotional barriers involve fear of doing something wrong and judging ideas instead of taking risks. Both of these behaviors can be seen in deep poverty as learned behavior from previous generations, which lead to two additional blocks: cultural and environmental (Evans, 1993). These are exhibited in neighborhoods that experience other characteristics related to deep poverty, such as violence, high crime rates, poor health, and failing schools. Environmental barriers are also exhibited in job pressures/lack of job opportunity, and time pressures. These may be exhibited in everyone's life but could be viewed as an additional layer of oppression that further inhibits creativity. This could present as feelings of helplessness in the face of such negativity.

An additional block is the fluency to express emotions appropriately. This may present in deep poverty as aggression, lashing out, and an inability to have others see you as an equal. As for intellectual blocks, they occur as a result of both lacking the skill and lacking the information necessary to solve a problem (Fogler, LeBlanc, & Rizzo, 2014).

Motivation is the determinate between what a creative individual is capable of doing and the choice of what will be done or not done (Hennessey, Moran, Altringer, & Amabile, 2015). In deep poverty, motivation may not be present due to stress, poor health, or lack of adequate food and water. As stated earlier, stress over circumstances may become paralyzing and lead to a feeling of helplessness. Those in deep poverty experience the same creativity blockers that the rest of us face. For some, these may appear as challenges each of us has overcome. In deep poverty, the challenges may appear insurmountable.

> The context of scarcity makes you myopic (exhibiting bias toward here and now). The mind is focused on present scarcity. We overvalue immediate benefits at the expense of future ones (e.g., procrastinate important things, such as medical checkups, or exercising). We only attend to urgent things and fail to make small investments even when future benefits can be substantial. To attend to the future requires cognitive resources, which scarcity depletes. (Heshmat, 2015)

Overall, the price of creativity may simply be too large both emotionally and financially for those in deep poverty.

Overcoming Poverty With Creativity

From 1959-1973, the poverty rate in the United States was cut in half due to changes in the economy, investments in family economic security, and civil rights protections (Vallas & Boteach, 2014). If deep poverty is generational, how is it that some manage to make great strides in their lives and others seem never to get ahead? Look at Oprah Winfrey, who spent her childhood wearing potato sacks because of lack of clothing, or Supreme Court Justice Sonia Sotomayor, who grew up in the South Bronx surrounded by crime and gangs (Robinson, 2014). When I think of these women, I think, *How did they achieve such great success?* They fought their way out of poverty. They were determined to get ahead. Others who achieved success despite deep poverty include Ursula Burns, CEO of Xerox , and Shawn Carter, also known as Jay-Z, who grew up in an area of New York that was dangerous and riddled with high crime rates (Werft, 2015). These individuals grew up poor and, through creativity, ingenuity, and education, became recognized influencers in the world. According to Werft (2015):

> Overcoming adversity develops qualities that humans often look to for guidance and leadership. Education and opportunity need to be accessible for disadvantaged youth before they can achieve the goals in life that are necessary to become leaders in communities. Most of the time, the burden of poverty proves too great.

There seems to be a direct correlation between drive and success, but why does poverty instill a drive in some individuals but hinder others? Is it in someone's nature to be more persistent or passive? Why do some let poverty serve as a catalyst for their dreams while others let poverty negatively shape their future? There seems to be a poverty or scarcity mindset that hinders those in deep poverty. Scarcity affects our thinking and feeling. Scarcity orients the mind automatically and powerfully toward unfulfilled needs (Heshmat, 2015).

There seem to be too many variables when it comes to creativity to say that those who live in poverty are more creative. I have read many articles that describe intellect, development, socioeconomic status, parental influence, birth order, adaptability, peer acceptance, and many other variables. The only conclusion that I can come to is an inconclusive one.

A Change in Government Policy

There is a need to change how deep poverty is viewed in the United States. Americans associate poverty with failure and have the mistaken belief that you can become wealthy through hard work (Cequea, 2018). This is not true. Poverty is a direct result of policy choices that put wealth and income in the hands of a few at the expense of growing a strong middle class (Vallas & Boteach, 2014). Compared to other nations, the United States is not progressive in its thinking regarding poverty and the disparity between the wealthy and the poor. There is a lack of economic mobility in the United States that has grown over the past four decades. Income inequality is on the rise (Cequea, 2018).

The government can enact policies that have worked in other nations, such as affordable education and a fair tax system. Affordable education, such as low-cost or free education, can increase a person's potential to get out of poverty by a factor of three (Cequea, n.d.). A fair tax system is where the wealthy are held accountable for their fair share of the tax burden. This is a matter of percentages rather than an exact number. An additional policy that can change, but has not, is universal access to basic needs such as healthcare. Most of the population of the United States is one accident or health tragedy away from medical bankruptcy (Cequea, n.d.). Other countries that have enacted universal healthcare have less economic disparity among its citizens.

The best way out of poverty is through a well-paying job and a livable wage. Most jobs offered to those in poverty have no upward mobility and have limited income growth. Another way is to increase the minimum wage. There also needs to be substantial investment in high-quality childcare and early education. The government needs to rebuild its infrastructure, renovate abandoned housing, revitalize neighborhoods, and make investments that create jobs. There is nothing inevitable about poverty. Unfortunately, 65% of people who are born into poverty will stay in poverty during their lifetimes (Cequea, n.d.). The government needs to enact policies that will increase economic security and expand opportunities (Vallas & Boteach, 2014).

Conclusion

I wanted to have my question regarding the connection of those in deep poverty and creativity answered, and I wanted it to be a resounding *Yes! They are more creative!* I thought there would be a clear answer. I found it to be so much more complicated. There are just too many variables to make a clear-cut determination regarding the creativity of those in deep poverty.

Those who live in deep poverty face many more creativity killers than those who do not. Unending stress, fear of failure, external pressures, self-limitations, and weighing the risks versus the rewards are overwhelming in deep poverty. On a positive note, there is a good chance that the divergent thinking abilities of those in poverty are more expansive, therefore making them more creative. In deep poverty, despite diverging to come up with a variety of solutions, only some are workable, and few are realistic. There is also the factor that those who live in deep poverty do not have the luxury of taking the time to find the right answer. The choices that have to be made are limited by internal and external influences as well as lack of funds. The choices are narrowed down until a person in deep poverty looks to old solutions that worked previously rather than look for new solutions. While new solutions may help, the attitude to go with what you know will not fail is safer than risking something that may drag you and/or your family into greater poverty or worse circumstances.

I was also hoping to find that my grandmother was more creative based on her lack of income. Was she creative? Yes, she was. She had a fifth-grade education but had a full creative life in which she made huge contributions to her community. Despite her lack of resources, she was a Boy Scout troop leader, she opened a well-child clinic in her neighborhood, and she did the crossword puzzle every day in pen. She was involved in politics, and she was well known and respected. When she was alive, a park was named after her, and when she passed, the City of Buffalo named a street after her. While I may not have found all of the answers in regard to creativity and deep poverty, I still feel that I had a great example on how to live a full creative life. My grandmother reached her own version of eminent creativity within her immediate community.

No one knows her outside the City of Buffalo, but those who live on Rosetta Petruzzi Way know her name. My grandmother may have lived in deep poverty but her creativity was notable and worthy of recognition, even if it is just by those whose lives were enriched by her resourcefulness. She did not let creativity-killers get in her way. She took risks, she was determined, she looked at all the options, and she did what she did for other people and not for herself. She never took no for an answer when it came to helping others. She never said an unkind word about anyone. She looked upon everyone as an equal even if others looked up to her. I think that her most notable contribution was that she lived a full, rich, creative life despite living in poverty.

References

Beghetto, R. A., & Kaufman, J. C. (2007). Toward a broader conception of creativity: A case for "mini-c" creativity. *Psychology of aesthetics, creativity, and the arts,* 1(2), 73-79. doi:10.1037/1931-3896.1.2.73

Benson, A. B. (2017, September 14). Library. Retrieved November 29, 2017, from https://www.census.gov/library/publications/2017/acs/acsbr16-01.html

Cequea, A. (n.d.). Economic inequality is a problem we can solve [Video]. *Act. tv.* Retrieved from http://act.tv/v/17210/

Cequea, A. (2018, January 19). Let's stop blaming poverty on the poor [Video]. *Social good now.* Retrieved from http://www.socialgoodnow.com/lets-stop-blaming-poverty-on-the-poor-video/#more-229

Cruze, R. (2017, July 06). The envelope system explained [Blog post]. *Dave Ramsey.* Retrieved from http://www.daveramsey.com/blog/envelope-system-explained

Evans, J. R. (1993). Creativity in MS/OR: Overcoming Barriers to Creativity. *Interfaces,* 23(6), 101-106.

Fogler, H. S, LeBlanc, S. E., & Rizzo, B. (2014). *Strategies for creative problem solving* (3rd edition). Upper Saddle River, NJ: Prentice Hall.

Gilliard, M. (n.d.). Barriers to creativity [Blog post]. Retrieved from http://www.innovation-creativity.com/barriers-to-creativity.html

Grebey, J. (2017, August 24). The 60 greatest kids' toys ever invented. *Business insider.* Retrieved from http://www.businessinsider.com/toys-in-the-national-toy-hall-of-fame-2016-7

Hennessey, B., Moran, S., Altringer, B., & Amabile, T. M. (2015). Extrinsic and intrinsic motivation. *Wiley encyclopedia of management,* 1-4.

Heshmat, S. (2015, April 2). The scarcity mindset. *Psychology today.* Retrieved from https://www.psychologytoday.com/blog/science-choice/201504/the-scarcity-mindset

Hill, R. P. (2001). Surviving in a material world: Evidence from ethnographic consumer research on people in poverty. *Journal of contemporary ethnography,* 30(4), 364-391. doi:10.1177/089124101030004002

Maslow, A. H. (1943). A theory of human motivation. *Psychological review,* 50(4), 370-396.

Mehta, R., & Zhu, M. (2016). Creating when you have less: The impact of resource scarcity on product use creativity. *Journal of consumer research,* 42(5), 767–782. doi:10.1093/jcr/ucv051

Ouellette, J. A., & Wood, W. (1998). Habit and intention in everyday life: The multiple processes by which past behavior predicts future behavior. *Psychological bulletin, 124*(1), 54-74.

Robinson, A. (2014, February 18). Powerful women that have overcome poverty [Blog post]. *The Borgen project*. Retrieved from https://borgenproject.org/powerful-women-overcome-poverty/

Runco, M. A. (2004). Creativity. *Annual Review of psychology, 55*(1), 657-687.

Runco, M. A. (2010). Divergent thinking, creativity and ideation. In J. C. Kaufman & R. J. Stenberg (Eds.), *The Cambridge handbook of creativity* (pp. 413-444). New York, NY: Cambridge University Press.

Samega, J., Fontenot K. R., & Kollar M. A. (2017). *Income and poverty in the United States: 2016*. (U.S. Census Bureau, Current Population Reports, P60-259). Retrieved from https://www.census.gov/content/dam/Census/library/publications/2017/demo/P60-259.pdf

Scopelliti, I., Cillo, P., Busacca, B., & Mazursky, D. (2014, September). How do financial constraints affect creativity? *The journal of product innovation management, 31*(5), 880-893. doi:10.1111/jpim.12129

Smith, K. L., Michael, W. B., & Hocevar, D. (2009). Performance on creativity measures with examination-taking instructions intended to induce high or low levels of test anxiety. *Creativity research journal, 3*(4), 265-280. doi:10.1080/1040041900953460

UC Davis Center for Poverty Research. (2017, December 18). *What is the current poverty rate in the United States?* Retrieved from https://poverty.ucdavis.edu/faq/what-current-poverty-rate-united-states

University of Illinois at Urbana-Champaign. (2015, November 17). Scarcity, not abundance, enhances consumer creativity, study says. *ScienceDaily*. Retrieved from http://www.sciencedaily.com/releases/2015/11/151117130342.htm

U.S. Census Bureau (2017, August 11). *How the Census Bureau measures poverty*. Retrieved from https://www.census.gov/topics/income-poverty/poverty/guidance/poverty-measures.html

Vallas, R., Boteach, M. (2014, September 17). The top 10 solutions to cut poverty and grow the middle class. *Center for American progress*. Retrieved from www.americanprogress.org/issues/poverty/news/2014/09/17/9728/the-top-10-solutions-to-cut-poverty-and-grow-the-middle-class/

Werft, M. (2015, October 22). 5 influential people who faced adversity growing up. *Global citizen*. Retrieved from https://www.globalcitizen.org/en/content/5-influential-people-who-faced-adversity-growing-u/

About the Author

Cher Ravenell is a graphic designer and is the director of publications at D'Youville College in Buffalo, New York. In her barely-existent free time, Cher is a freelance designer, writer, teacher, and creative consultant for many individuals, groups and companies in the Western New York area. Her consultant work allows her to do what she loves twice a year: Lay on a beach in Riviera Maya, Mexico, with a café con leche wearing SPF 50. Questioning everything and everyone, Cher shows a strong interest in links to creativity and poverty as well as an interest in fostering the creative female. Cher holds a bachelor's degree in management for not-for-profits from the State University of New York, and a master's degree in creativity from the International Center for Studies in Creativity at SUNY Buffalo State. Cher lives in Buffalo with her husband Eugene, and has four daughters including twins, a pug named Zsa Zsa Gabor, and a beast of a cat named Clark Gable.

Acknowledgments

We would like to thank Paul Reali at ICSC Press for his hard work and dedication in bringing the *Big Questions in Creativity* books to life and helping us to sustain it over the last six years. Also, to Kevin Opp, who designed a book that is polished and reader-friendly.

We wish to express our gratitude to our copy editors Julia Figliotti and Joshua Gordon, whose mastery of language and attention to detail have made them assets to this project.

Our colleagues at the International Center for Studies in Creativity at SUNY Buffalo State deserve special thanks. Gerard Puccio, Creative Studies department chair, and Rita Zientek, associate dean of the School of Professions, have supported the ICSC Press since its inception. Selcuk Acar, John Cabra, Roger Firestien, J. Michael Fox, Sue Keller-Mathers, and Jo Yudess continue to challenge the students of the ICSC and inspire both the asking of questions, and the persistence of curiosity.

We are grateful to our families and friends for their encouragement, especially Ryan Fields and Andy Burnett.

And finally, our deepest appreciation and admiration goes to the contributors to *Big Questions in Creativity 2018*. They are the new torch bearers for the mission of the ICSC to ignite creativity around the world.

About the Editors

Kristin Fields is a Training Coordinator with the Center for Development of Human Services (CDHS), Institute for Community Health Promotion, SUNY Buffalo State. In this role, she is administrator of a training contract focused on the development of management and supervisory skills, as well as trainer skill development. Kristin also serves as an internal facilitator for strategic initiatives and coordinates professional development opportunities for all CDHS staff.

In addition to her work at CDHS, Kristin is adjunct faculty for the Creative Studies department at SUNY Buffalo State, as well as the designer/instructor of the Entrepreneurial Effectiveness program, run through the Small Business Development Center, also of SUNY Buffalo State. Career highlights include a publication in the Journal of Museum Education on encouraging and supporting creativity, as well as the facilitation of numerous workshops on such topics as developing mission and vision statements and engaging adult learners. Kristin is a certified facilitator of The 7 Habits of Highly Effective People Signature Program. She holds a Bachelor of Science degree in Speech Language Pathology and a Master of Science degree in Creativity and Innovation, both from SUNY Buffalo State.

Email: fieldsfacilitator@outlook.com
Linked In: https://www.linkedin.com/in/kristindaleyfields

Dr. Cyndi Burnett is an Associate Professor at the International Center for Studies in Creativity at Buffalo State. She has a Master of Science in Creativity, and a Doctorate of Education in Curriculum, Teaching and Learning, all of which she uses to help "ignite creativity around the world." Her research interests include: the use of creative models and techniques with children, creative thinking in higher education, and current trends in creativity. Her work includes projects such as: working with educators to bring creative thinking into the classroom, connecting communities of creative thinkers via social media, and designing and running a Massive Open Online Course (MOOC) on Everyday Creativity. Dr. Burnett was featured in an article in the New York Times titled, "Creativity Becomes an Academic Discipline." She is the co-editor of the *Big Questions in Creativity* book series and co-author of the books *Weaving Creativity into Every Strand of Your Curriculum* and *My Sandwich is a Spaceship: Creative Thinking for Parents and Young Children*.

Web: cyndiburnett.com
Twitter: @CyndiBurnett
Facebook: https://www.facebook.com/cyndiaburnett/
Email: argonac@buffalostate.edu

Marie Mance is the Associate Director of the International Center for Studies in Creativity at SUNY Buffalo State where she has taught graduate and undergraduate creativity courses. Previously at Buffalo State, Marie was the Director of Leadership Development and Manager of Organizational Development. In addition to designing and coordinating the leadership program for academic leaders, she designed and delivered workshops and served as a coach. Marie holds an M.S. in Creativity and an M.Ed. in Counseling/Student Personnel. She has published a number of articles and book chapters on creativity and leadership and is the co-author of *Creative Leadership: Skills that Drive Change* and *Creativity Rising: Creative Thinking and Creative Problem Solving the in the 21st Century.*

About the International Center for Studies in Creativity

The International Center for Studies in Creativity (ICSC) is known around the world for its personally transformative undergraduate, graduate and distance programs that cultivate skills in creative thinking, innovative leadership practices and problem solving skills.

ICSC is the first program in the world to teach the science of creativity at a graduate level: Our Graduate Certificate program includes six courses that focus on creative process, facilitation, assessment, training, theory and leadership. With an additional four courses, including a master's project or thesis, students can complete a Master of Science degree in creativity and change leadership. Graduate students can pursue their degree on campus or via the distance program, which offers a blend of on-campus and virtual classrooms.

For 50 years, ICSC is proud to have contributed to seminal research to the field of creativity. ICSC is part of Buffalo State, The State University of New York.

To learn more, please visit creativity.buffalostate.edu.

About ICSC Press

Created in 2012, ICSC Press is the imprint of the International Center for Studies in Creativity. The mission of the press supports the vision of the Center to ignite creativity around the world, facilitating the recognition of creative thinking as an essential life skill. ICSC Press's goal is to put the work of our best teachers, thinkers, and practitioners into the hands of a wide audience, making titles available quickly and in multiple formats, both paper and electronic. Our titles include:

Books

Big Questions in Creativity 2017, Mary Kay Culpepper, Cynthia Burnett, & Paul D. Reali, Eds.

Big Questions in Creativity 2016, Paul D. Reali & Cynthia Burnett, Eds.

Why Study Creativity? Reflections & Lessons from the International Center for Studies in Creativity, Jon Michael Fox & Ronni Lea Fox, Eds.

My Sandwich is a Spaceship, by Cyndi Burnett & Michaelene Dawson-Globus

Big Questions in Creativity 2015, Mary Kay Culpepper & Cynthia Burnett, Eds.

Big Questions in Creativity 2014, Mary Kay Culpepper & Cynthia Burnett, Eds.

Big Questions in Creativity 2013, Cynthia Burnett & Paul D. Reali, Eds.

Creativity Rising: Creative Thinking and Creative Problem Solving in the 21st Century, by Gerard J. Puccio, Marie Mance, Laura Barbero Switalski, & Paul D. Reali

Journals

Business Creativity and the Creative Economy, Mark A. Runco, Ed.

Journal of Genius and Eminence, Mark A. Runco, Ed.

To learn more, to purchase titles, or to submit a proposal, visit icscpress.com.

www.ingramcontent.com/pod-product-compliance
Lightning Source LLC
Chambersburg PA
CBHW020058020526
44112CB00031B/361